SILENT VOICES

SECOND EDITION

PEOPLE WITH MENTAL DISORDERS ON THE STREET

ROBERT L. OKIN, MD

For more information, contact: www.goldenpinepress.com

Ordering Information:
Quantity sales. Special discounts are available on quantity purchases by corporations, associations, and others. For details, contact the "Special Sales Department" at the address above.

Orders by U.S. trade bookstores and wholesalers.
Please contact BCH: (800) 431-1579 or visit www.bookch.com for details.

All photos are courtesy of the author.

Cataloging-in-Publication data

Names: Okin, Robert L., author.
Title: Silent voices : people with mental disorders on the street , second edition / Robert
    L. Okin, MD.
Description: Includes bibliographical references and index. | Pope Valley, CA: Golden
    Pine Press, 2023.
Identifiers: LCCN: 2023903285 | ISBN: 978-0-99607771-2
Subjects: LCSH Homeless persons--California--San Francisco. | Homeless persons--
    California--San Francisco--Pictorial works. | Mentally ill homeless persons--
    California--San Francisco. | Mentally ill homeless persons--California--San
    Francisco--Pictorial works. | BISAC SOCIAL SCIENCE / Poverty & Homelessness
    | SOCIAL SCIENCE / Social Classes & Economic Disparity
Classification: LCC HV4506.S355 O55 2023 | DDC 362.309794/61--dc23

Printed in the United States of America on acid-free paper.

27 26 25 24 23   10 9 8 7 6 5 4 3 2 1

This book is dedicated to the generous people on the street who believed their voices and images could make a difference in the world. Without their willingness to speak out and share themselves with me, this book would not have been possible.

And to the brave families of some of these people who have fought a never-ending battle for the people they love, in both the personal and political spheres.

AUTHOR'S NOTE

I approached most of the people I interviewed for this book more or less randomly, and without a prior introduction. Some were referred to me by their social workers. To ensure informed consent, I explained to each person that I wished to photograph him or her and obtain a first-person narrative about his or her life for inclusion in a book I was writing. I asked whether the person would be interested in participating in the project. I requested consent both before and after conducting each interview or taking photographs. Thus, the person had an opportunity to withdraw his or her consent after hearing and answering my questions or having photographs taken. Only those individuals who consented both before *and* after the interview and the photography are included here. The individuals whose photographs appear on pages 57–61, 130, and 169 gave their consent to be photographed for the book but were not interviewed. Thus, although I encountered them on the street, I do not know for certain whether they were homeless or mentally ill.

CONTENTS

CAUSES OF CHRONIC HOMELESSNESS 205

SOLUTIONS.. 253

PREFACE

We avert our eyes when we pass them but can't help seeing them nonetheless. In fact, walking through many cities without encountering mentally ill people living on the streets is impossible. These people are the casualties of a society that blames, fears, impoverishes, segregates, and marginalizes them. If we bother to look, what we tend to see are the ways they are different from us, not the things we have in common. We don't recognize that they, like us, get cold when the temperature drops, wet when it rains on them, hungry when they haven't eaten, and exhausted when they can't find someplace comfortable to sleep. This failure to recognize our common humanity is the first step in a process of dehumanization that ultimately ensures that we sit by and allow our governments to enact policies and budgets that drive these people onto the streets and keep them there.

After encountering many people who were mentally ill and homeless both in the hospital where I worked for many years and on the streets, I found myself wondering how these people had become homeless and what factors kept them virtually imprisoned there. I wanted to understand the choices they made in their lives and how they coped in unbearably grim circumstances with nothing to their names but the clothes on their backs and the carts they pushed around the city. I wanted to learn what they were like as people beyond their rags, carts, tin cups, and strange behaviors. I decided to spend two years on the streets getting to know those who would talk to me. After numerous conversations, I wanted to share what I learned with a broader audience. The first-person narratives and photographs that grew from these conversations became the body of this book. The first section includes my experience in interviewing these people and summarizes what they told me about the reality of being homeless.

Each of the people presented here followed his or her own path in life, driven by widespread generic social forces as well as unique personal ones. The interaction of the individual and structural forces pushed the most vulnerable of these people onto the streets. Whereas the first part of the book focuses on the individual, the second half begins with a description of the underlying generic forces. Among them are the way deinstitutionalization was carried out in this country, the ravages of the drug epidemic, and the financial incentives that came to influence the admission and discharge practices of general hospitals. Adding to these factors were the growing tendency of cities and states to criminalize mental illness and homelessness; the severe shortage of affordable housing in many cities; the lack of a robust national social safety net, which virtually ensures the impoverishment of a large swath of the population; mental health programs that are completely inadequate to the task of caring for these people; cultural attitudes that shape the way we stigmatize them; and the dramatic failure of our foster care system that turns many of its "graduates" onto the streets either as soon as they become emancipated or years later.

Following the discussion of the causes of homelessness among mentally ill people is a chapter describing solutions to the problem. It seems obvious that homeless mentally ill people first and foremost need homes. And yet, despite the fact that the crisis of homelessness has been rampant in our cities for over fifty years, governments have failed miserably to create the number of low-cost affordable housing units needed to prevent people from slipping onto the street or to help those who have already slipped. Without the existence of such housing, no other solution will work. Had governments taken real action rather than hiding behind a litany of halfway measures, they would have solved the problem years ago. At the present rate of housing development, we will never catch up with the number of people presently on the street, much less prevent new people from becoming homeless.

Beyond developing affordable housing, governments must create targeted mental health services that help people apply for government benefits, link them to other services, support them through their inevitable crises, motivate them to take their medications, and guide them to develop lives that are meaningful and productive. These services must be adequately funded if we want clinicians to be able to do what their clients need. If we can develop both housing and services and mitigate some of the other causes of the problem, we will be able to stem the flow of people onto the streets—from the foster care system; from single-room occupancy (SRO) apartments; and from general hospitals, jails, and prisons.

As I finished my interviews on the street, I found myself filled with admiration and gratitude toward the people who spoke to me. I often wondered whether I could have survived what they endure every day and every night had I been living in their shoes. To a large degree, this book is a testimony to their bravery and tenacity. It is my hope that it will help readers see these troubled, profoundly impoverished people with more understanding and compassion and with less blame, fear, and anger.

SCOPE OF THE PROBLEM

PREVALENCE OF HOMELESSNESS IN OUR SOCIETY

The United States is facing a crisis of enormous proportions, and it is growing year by year. Hundreds of thousands of its citizens have no place to sleep, no place to eat, and no way to get out of the freezing rain. They are the wanderers of our society, the homeless mentally ill. And the problems they face in simply getting through their days and nights extend far beyond these individuals for they touch the rest of us as well.

Who are they? According to the US Department of Housing and Urban Development (2021),

- Of the 580,000 people who are homeless on any given night, 230,000, or 40 percent, are mentally ill or struggling with drugs or both.
- Approximately 200,000 people (35 percent) are living completely unsheltered on the street, representing a 7 percent increase between 2019 and 2020.
- Approximately 87,000 people (21 percent) are chronically homeless, signifying that they have a disabling condition and have been homeless for either at least one year or if less than this, then at least four shorter periods in the last three years. This represents an increase of 15 percent between 2019 and 2020.

- Approximately 184,000 of homeless people (32 percent) live in families, most of whom have been pushed onto the streets by financial reverses.
- Approximately 41,000 veterans are homeless largely due to the emotional wounds of war coupled with financial hardship.
- Approximately 34,000 are unaccompanied youth under the age of twenty-five.
- Women represent 39 percent of the homeless population, and half attribute their homelessness to partner violence.

The association of homelessness and race is particularly striking. As in so many other areas of American life, historically marginalized groups are more likely to be disadvantaged in the housing market. Systemic racism expressed in higher unemployment rates, lower incomes, public education that is compromised by inequities of local funding, less access to health care, redlining in the mortgage sector, and higher incarceration rates are some of the factors likely contributing to higher rates of homelessness among people of color. Below is a breakdown of some of the data related to homelessness and race:

- Black Americans, who represent 12 percent of the general population, constitute 39 percent of the homeless population and 53 percent of people experiencing homelessness as members of families with children.
- Native Hawaiians and other Pacific Islanders have the highest rate of homelessness (109 out of every 10,000 people in these groups) compared to the overall rate of homelessness, which is 18 out of every 10,000 people.

- Taken together, American Indian, Native Alaskan, Pacific Islander, and Native Hawaiian populations account for 5 percent of the homeless population and 7 percent of the unsheltered population but only 1 percent of the general population.
- People who identify as Hispanic or Latino make up about 23 percent of the homeless population but only 16 percent of the population overall.

COST OF HOMELESSNESS TO SOCIETY

Beyond the destructive effects of homelessness on the mentally ill individual, the cost to society is enormous. Multiple studies have demonstrated that ignoring the problem is twice as expensive as treating it by providing these people housing and support services. A New York City study of 4,679 homeless people with severe mental illness demonstrated that it costs approximately $40,000 per year to leave a homeless mentally ill person on the street but only $24,000 to provide housing and supportive services to him (Culhane et al., 2002). It costs the San Francisco Department of Public Works over $30 million each year to simply pick up the 120,000 thousand needles discarded by people with substance abuse disorders and to scrape the feces off the sidewalks deposited by homeless people who often have nowhere else to defecate. Other studies have demonstrated that keeping someone homeless costs about $40,000–80,000 versus providing decent housing and ancillary services, which costs $20,000–$30,000 (National Alliance to End Homelessness, 2017).

The reason that the costs of homelessness are not widely appreciated is that they are buried in the budgets of many different city departments and require analysis to disaggregate. For example, the cost of picking up needles and scraping feces off the streets can be found in the budget of public works departments. The cost of bringing homeless people to the emergency room is hidden in police and ambulance budgets. The cost of treating people during acute psychiatric episodes is buried in general hospital budgets. The costs of apprehending and jailing homeless people, usually for minor crimes, are hidden in the budgets of the police, courts, and jails. For any particular person, these costs escalate quickly, and we as citizens end up paying for them.

But another cost of homelessness affects all of us. We are all forced to face the pain that we, by our negligence and political apathy, inflict on people who often and through no fault of their own end up on the streets. We might avoid looking at them when we pass them by, but the tragedy of their lives inevitably affects us, even if subliminally. These people stand as a mirror to our collective guilt.

How this Project Began

I was sitting on a bench near the Ferry Building in San Francisco, waiting for a friend and watching the sun come up over the bay, when a middle-aged black man sat down next to me. I had seen him a few minutes earlier pushing a shopping cart loaded with his clothes, sleeping bag, and other possessions. Despite the eighty-five-degree heat, he was covered in several layers of thick woolen clothing and was completely hooded. Only his eyes were visible. As I turned to him, he began whispering silently to himself and then to the bell that clanged in the tower of the Ferry Building at fifteen-minute intervals. "Who are you talking to?" I asked him. "God," he responded. "How do you get in touch with him?" I pursued. "Through the bell," he whispered and abruptly stood up and walked away, pushing his cart in front of him.

A few minutes later, I watched a woman dressed in rags, with nothing on her feet, pulling a train of three carts loaded with what seemed like odds and ends. She stopped suddenly in the middle of the street, gesticulated wildly to the passing traffic, and went on her way.

In the next half hour, I saw a blue sleeping bag floating down the sidewalk. The young woman inside of it dug into each trash can along her path. Occasionally, she'd find a half-finished, discarded cup of coffee and would drink what was left of it. I walked up to her and offered to take her to a coffee shop around the corner. She came with me and told me she'd come to San Francisco from Italy for a vacation but couldn't remember from which city or when. After nibbling on a bun, like a little mouse,

she excused herself politely and walked out. I saw her several times after that, walking around the area, dragging her sleeping bag behind her, never talking to anyone. On one occasion, she disrobed in the middle of the public square, replacing her sweatshirt with a lighter garment.

I found myself totally absorbed by these people as they made their way silently around the city. I had been interested in people with severe mental illness throughout my professional career, from the time I was commissioner of mental health for the states of Vermont and Massachusetts through my seventeen years as chief of psychiatry at San Francisco General Hospital and professor of clinical psychiatry at University of California, San Francisco. In each of these positions, I designed programs for severely mentally ill people so they could live with dignity in the community. While most people, with this support, could be treated outside the walls of hospitals, budgetary constraints prevented us from developing the programs necessary to reach all the people who needed help.

Even with my considerable experience, I was always bewildered by how the mentally ill living on the street managed to survive when programs were unavailable to them. When I retired from my position at the hospital, I decided to find out. I wanted to get closer to these people in order to hear from them about their lives directly and personally. I wanted to understand how they coped with their illnesses and the stresses of homelessness and jail. I wanted to know what they thought about as they pushed their carts down the street, what they did with their empty time, how they managed at night, and why they made some of the choices they did. I wanted to know how they dealt with being "moved along" or arrested by the police when they were discovered sleeping on park benches. I wanted to know how they dealt with being so utterly shunned by society.

I wanted to know how they showered, where they relieved themselves when there were no public toilets at hand, and how some developed the motivation to get off drugs when life on the street was so stressful, barren, and discouraging, and when there was nothing else to look forward to but the next fix. I wanted to understand why they so often refused to take their psychiatric medications, why some preferred to live outside in the cold and rain than in shelters or transient hotels, and why in the world any of them would choose to live in foggy San Francisco rather than balmy San Diego or Los Angeles. In a sense, I wanted to see these people beyond their rags, their carts, their tin cups, and their strange behaviors. I wanted to see the ways they were the same as I was, not just the ways they were different.

I decided to leave my office in the hospital and meet these people where they lived. I approached people who appeared to be homeless and mentally ill and asked them if they would speak to me about their lives—their joys, sorrows, struggles, and triumphs. I wanted to understand what it was like to live in their skin and walk in their shoes, enveloped in so much isolation and silence. I decided to spend time with them on the street, in their rooms, in court, and in shelters. This was the only way I was going to get the kind of nitty-gritty knowledge I was seeking. It was the only way I was going to understand what life was like from their point of view.

MY APPROACH TO THIS PROJECT

My original plan was simply to start up conversations with people I met on the street, hope they wouldn't think I was too weird, and ask them if they would talk to me about their lives. But after a few encounters, I was so intrigued and moved by some of their stories that I developed a wish to share them with a larger audience. I wanted to convey the human face of mental disorders as a counterweight to the fear, hostility, and indifference with which mentally ill people are generally seen and portrayed. By giving them a voice in the public domain, I wanted to enable them to convey their longings, regrets, joys, anxieties, hopes—their essential humanity.

My initial intention was to focus on people who were presumptively diagnosable with mental disorders, at least from my observations on the street. But in time, it became clear to me, as it had in clinical contexts, that a very large number of people I met didn't fit neatly into formal diagnostic categories. Nevertheless, many of them were extremely troubled; were doing poorly in their lives by any standard; and were suffering from some combination of genetic vulnerability, difficult family situations, childhood abuse, traumas of war, drug addiction, poverty, and social marginalization. Most seemed to be missing certain crucial capacities needed to function normally in society. It was people within this broader definition of what it means to be mentally ill that I decided to include in this book. Some of the individuals I chose to interview were involved in mental health programs and were referred to me by their social workers. The vast majority, however, I approached directly and spontaneously on the street without any introduction.

I always talked to people privately, though often in relatively public places—standing or sitting on a street corner or in a coffee shop, subway station, or park. Early in my interactions with these individuals, I was struck by the beauty and expressiveness of their faces as they deeply and authentically told me about their lives. So I began asking people if I could take their photographs while we were talking. I decided not to pose them in front of a black or white background even though this might have led to greater artistic effect, because I didn't want to decontextualize them from the physical circumstances of their lives. When choices had to be made, I strove for authenticity over drama.

My Experience on the Street

When I first went onto the street, I wasn't certain I would be able to engage people to participate, especially when I explained that I wished to record their narratives and take their photographs while they spoke to me. I discovered, however, that most of the people I met agreed to participate, frequently after I was able to overcome their initial mistrust, anxiety, shame, and anger. Many were willing to talk to me with surprising candor and feeling about very intimate issues. They often spoke with tears in their eyes.

AN ETHICAL DILEMMA

Especially at times of intense emotion, I was concerned about how probing to be, even though these people had given me explicit consent to record and photograph them. Had this consent really been informed? I sometimes asked myself. Had they really known what they were getting into? Did they really want

their voices to be heard when they were conveying stories that were so intimate and potentially so embarrassing? Regarding informed consent, I was careful to ask for consent both before and after conducting an interview or taking photographs. Thus, the person had an opportunity to withdraw his or her consent after hearing and answering my questions or having photographs taken. Only those individuals who consented both before *and* after the interview or the photography are included here. (I describe my consent methodology in greater detail in the Author's Note at the beginning of the book.) Beyond the issue of formal consent, it seemed disrespectful, unfeeling, intrusive, and incredibly awkward to raise the camera between us and click the shutter at these vulnerable moments, recording forever the images of their distress. Yet my wish to convey to readers the depth of feeling so many mentally ill people were silently bearing, buried under their more visible symptoms, was one of the main reasons for the project. It was this very depth of feeling that I hoped readers might relate to.

Although my intent was fundamentally altruistic, I was often haunted by a concern that I was spying into the misery of other people's lives partially out of my own voyeuristic interest. I was often worried that I was using, exposing, and exploiting people whom life had already treated so poorly. I was a total stranger, yet I was asking people to expose their personal lives to me and to the public, even when this might be painful and, in some cases, humiliating. It is hardly surprising that, at times, I felt I had no right to be on the street and that the enterprise was somehow illegitimate, even though I had diligently obtained the consent of the people I was writing about.

WHY THEY PARTICIPATED

I began to feel more comfortable in my interviews as I recognized that most of the people who agreed to participate felt that they were receiving something in return—the possibility of being seen and heard, by me and perhaps by others, and of having some kind of impact in the world. Many participants had never been listened to as children, felt voiceless and invisible as adults, and were certain that no one would notice or miss them when they were gone. Having their words and images recorded seemed to give them tangible evidence that the universe had taken note of their existence, that they would leave their footprints in the sand. For some people, participating fulfilled a deep wish to do something they regarded as socially useful—to warn, to teach, to inspire, and to demonstrate that it was possible to do something constructive in the world. They shared their experiences to counter both their own and society's perception of them as useless—or worse, destructive.

Those individuals who had been referred to me by mental health programs universally expressed the hope that by participating, they could give back to staff members who had truly cared about them—and even, in some cases, saved their lives. For these people, participation was an act of public gratitude, an opportunity to pay tribute to the staff's work in a very personal way.

GOOD DAYS AND BAD DAYS

In the early days of the project, I was very anxious. One reason was that I felt like the ultimate outsider, the well-heeled, camera-toting guy who clearly didn't belong on the street. Being on the street gave me a small taste of what it was like to be "the other." The sense of being different, of not fitting in, was extremely disturbing on some primal level, despite the fact that some of the ways I was different obviously gave me certain advantages in life. Moreover, I was the supplicant, the one who needed help and cooperation rather than the person who could give these things. I was the one asking for a handout—in the form of photographs and stories. I was the panhandler with the tin cup who could be ignored, derided, or dismissed. This was the worst part of the whole experience for me.

Although people were generally very friendly to me, there were some painful exceptions. Sometimes they regarded me with a degree of mistrust that I was unable to break through, and they dismissed me with a wave of the hand. This was particularly the case when a lot of methamphetamine was available on the street. More people than usual were high, irritable, suspicious, volatile, and very crazy. At these times, I was afraid that even looking at someone too directly might be experienced as provocative and lead to an angry eruption. Perhaps because I was careful, this never happened to me in any serious way, though I had a couple of trivial encounters. On one occasion, a young man saw me photographing someone, believed I hadn't asked permission, and concluded I was being disrespectful. He hurled an apple at me, catching me in the chest. He later apologized when I confronted him about it. In another instance, a woman became suddenly and unexpectedly angry about my approaching her, picked up her crutch, and threatened me with it.

I met several people who were difficult to understand because their thoughts were so scrambled and delusional. These people might have been easily dismissed as "crazy" because they seemed to be living in internal worlds that were intensely dangerous and infuriating. Frequently, the people who appeared to be the most enraged and explosive were also the most scared. Some of them may, in fact, have been hurt or invaded earlier in their lives, and were expressing their enduring reactions to these experiences in the only language they knew. Being with these people was always an unsettling experience, the more so when I was finally able to pick disturbing themes out of their confusing thoughts.

I often felt exhausted and drained at the end of the day and couldn't imagine how I was going to get back onto the street again the next morning. Wandering around in the absence of a clear-cut agenda often felt aimless and unfocused. I often wondered how the people I met could tolerate this kind of life as their steady diet. Occasionally, after spending time with people who were very disorganized and psychotic, I felt disoriented and off-balance myself. Even when people spoke to me in a way I understood, I frequently found what they said disturbing. Their stories of bleakness and misfortune often left me with a lump in my throat and an overwhelming sense of loneliness, isolation, and despair. At these times, I couldn't seem to separate my life from theirs, and felt only an inch away from falling off the same edge that had crumbled beneath their feet.

Lest I convey the impression that my experience on the street was mostly anxious or sad, I need to emphasize how many "good days" I had. Most people I talked to were welcoming, interesting, and smart; made me feel comfortable; and conveyed their belief that I was engaged in something valuable. Some people were funny and entertaining, seemed to genuinely enjoy their lives, and showed me a different side to my own. Equally pleasurable was being challenged by new experiences and forced to question certain cherished assumptions. Best of all, and a bonus that has lasted long after the conclusion of the project, were enduring friendships with several of the people I met.

PERSONAL INVOLVEMENT

Almost as soon as I began meeting people, I struggled with the question of how involved to become in their lives. Taking a detached and "objective" position, assuming a more classically anthropological approach, limiting myself to observing, recording, bearing witness, and in a sense remaining on the outside of their experience, seemed to undermine my original intention of understanding their lives more deeply. My decision was ultimately influenced less by these intellectual considerations than by my inability to resist the pull to become involved with certain people who welcomed me into their lives. In some cases, it seemed simply like the right thing to do. In other cases, I became quite attached to them and felt nourished by the give and take, informality, mutual acceptance, and ease of the relationship.

I tried to help some of these people with the issues they were struggling with, sometimes to good effect and sometimes to no effect. There are few experiences so illuminating, and so humbling, as trying to help someone solve an apparently simple practical problem, and failing miserably. Notwithstanding these failures when they occurred, I was always surprised at how simple acts of human kindness could make such a seemingly large difference. Although I may have sacrificed a certain amount of objectivity by my real-life involvement, I believe that I gained a much deeper understanding of people's lives than would have been possible with a more detached approach.

Contributing to my initial anxiety were my negative judgments of the people I was talking to—the very judgments I was struggling against. The result was that I initially couldn't figure out how to explain the project to the people I approached in a way they were likely to view as respectful and supportive, rather than shaming and denigrating. However artfully I put my request, I feared they would detect my underlying critique, as though I was saying, "Excuse me, sir, I'm interested in talking with you because you look so colorfully beaten up by life, like you can't cope." Or, "Excuse me, ma'am, you look like a real screw-up who's made a total mess of your life. It would really be fascinating to hear about how you accomplished this. Moreover, with your permission, I'd love to spread the story of your unhappy life, along with your picture, all over the public domain. Would that be okay?" Was it any wonder I expected people to turn me down?

As I got to know certain people, the negative stereotypes I was secretly harboring (and the fears I had of people's negative stereotypes of me) gradually melted away. Making contact with these individuals and hearing their stories helped me genuinely appreciate what most of them had been up against from the day they were born, and what they were still dealing with day after day. Even when I saw how they were actively contributing to their unhappy lives, something that used to infuriate me, I began to understand why they were doing it. I could see that their "bad" choices were driven by forces that felt irresistible to them. With experience and exposure, my original judgments were replaced by admiration, and by the nagging and uncomfortable question of how I would have fared with the miserable hand that life had dealt them.

Paths to Becoming Mentally Ill and Homeless

This book presents the stories of people who are both mentally ill and homeless. Most people with mental illness do not become homeless. But mental illness can lead to homelessness when people's symptoms become so severe that their functioning is impaired. Their resulting poverty pushes them onto the street. Conversely, the stresses of homelessness increase the likelihood that someone on the margin of mental illness will be forced over the edge. It is the particular interaction between biological vulnerability, severe environmental experiences, and street drugs that can lead to both mental illness and homelessness.

Some people I interviewed probably came into the world genetically vulnerable to mental illness. Others were abused and neglected at an early age. Unable to concentrate as a result, many began failing in school and turned to drugs, which complicated their learning problems. Some developed mental illness in late adolescence or early adulthood as a result of one or several of these factors. Failing to graduate from high school, whatever the cause, many entered adulthood without marketable skills and never made it into the job market. Without an early employment history, they had nothing to parlay into future job opportunities. Others, even if they managed to get through adolescence without obvious symptoms, suffered some trauma or serious reversal as adults (for example, warfare experiences or significant personal losses), turned to drugs to numb their intense emotional reactions to these events, and became symptomatic.

CHILDHOOD TRAUMAS

The vast majority of people I spoke to had experienced multiple traumas in childhood. Most had parents who were neglectful, drug-addicted, and abusive. Some parents were severely mentally ill. The individuals I interviewed relayed accounts of being regularly beaten, verbally assaulted, or abandoned as children. Many lived in constant fear for their safety. Some were drawn into the drug culture by older siblings or their own parents, some of whom were using or addicted to drugs. The mother of one man I met was so violent that on separate occasions, she shot her husband and heaved him through a plate-glass window. The father of another put his son's feet to a fire, severely burning him for misbehaving.

Almost half of the homeless mentally ill women I met had been sexually abused as children, sometimes violently. Whereas I had expected that many would have experienced sexual abuse and maternal neglect, I was unprepared for how prevalent this was. Many turned to drugs and promiscuous sex in adolescence to blunt the painful emotional consequences of these early experiences, but these choices set them up for further sexual and emotional abuse. Most became homeless through their use of drugs, economic catastrophe, psychiatric symptoms, or the belief that they deserved nothing better in life.

Whatever their genetic vulnerability, it was clear that childhood traumas and sexual abuse had also permanently wounded the people I talked to, truncated their emotional development, and led to pervasive functional deficits in adulthood. It is easy to forget the impact of such experiences when we pass these people on the street, especially when all we can see are the outward signs of their poverty and their odd conduct. In fact, it is easy to forget they were children at all.

DRUG ADDICTION

The lives of a large number of the people I met in the course of writing this book revolved around getting, using, and recovering from drugs. For most of these people, several factors converged to perpetuate their drug use, making drugs almost irresistible. These factors included a biological vulnerability to addiction, identification with parents who used, neglect and abuse in childhood, involvement in drug-using social networks in adolescence, extreme poverty in adulthood, and an inability to cope with painful feelings of depression, anxiety, rage, boredom, psychotic symptoms, and posttraumatic stress.

The majority of people who resorted to alcohol and drugs as a consistent part of their lives dug themselves into a pit of unemployability. Both the altered states of consciousness these substances brought about in the short term and the personality changes they caused in the long term sapped these individuals' mental and physical energy, and killed their drive and ambition. Drugs made it almost impossible for them to plan, organize, remember, get themselves to places on time, execute their intentions, and handle the interpersonal stress associated with even low-level jobs. The impairment of these functions was further compromised by other symptoms of mental disorder. Once they began living on the street, many became ensnared in a cycle of homelessness and joblessness.

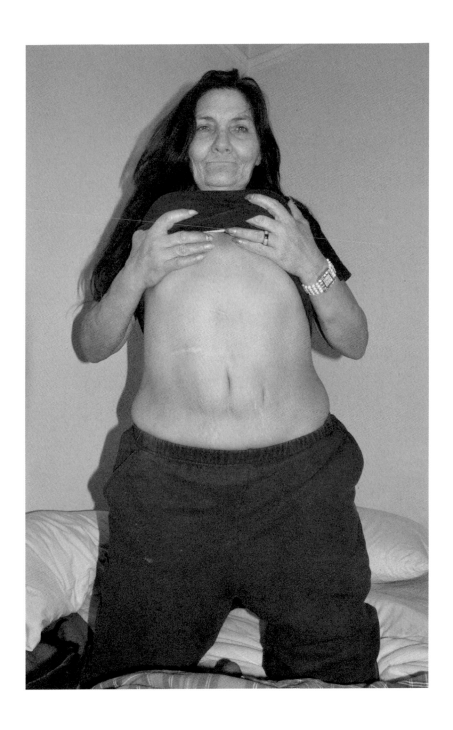

Several individuals had spent time in jail or prison for possession and sale of drugs, and some for theft they engaged in to maintain their addictions. One man stole $200 worth of merchandise every day to support his habit. He was jailed three times and only escaped going to prison for a year through the intervention of his social worker. Some of the women used prostitution to pay for drugs. Almost everyone I spoke to had several friends who had died from drug overdoses or other complications of addiction.

Given the destructiveness of drugs, it is natural to wonder why people don't just stop using, as if getting off were simply an act of will. Some individuals seem to find the inner strength to quit, but often they have to reach a point of desperation first. Those people I spoke to who escaped from the drug life were able to do so only with the help of specialized treatment programs—and when they were looking death in the eye. Drugs are an almost inescapable way of numbing oneself to the hardships of life on the street, and giving them up by oneself is almost impossible. As one man put it, "Living on the street is so bad, you have to be either stoned or crazy to bear it."

PERSONAL LOSSES

I expected to encounter impenetrability, hardened shells, and resistance when I asked people on the street about their lives, but the majority seemed genuinely to welcome the chance to unburden themselves to another person. Most were coping with intense grief about very painful issues in their lives and had been unable to resolve the losses and traumas that had occurred often many years before. I was totally unprepared for how close to the surface these feelings were. No matter how "tough" these people first appeared, they became openly tearful at some point during our talks. They evinced sadness, regret, rage, depression, and guilt over personal calamities such as betrayal by a spouse, firing from a job, abandonment by a parent, or death of a spouse or child. These losses, along with the other issues they were coping with, led to a collapse in their ability to function and ultimately to their state of homelessness.

BARELY GETTING BY

Most of the people I spoke to were barely getting by, if that. Sometimes they were able to sustain themselves on the street through government subsidies, but often they survived through a variety of ingenious, if sometimes illegal, means. Some of them traded prescribed medications for street drugs. Others prostituted for money or drugs, shoplifted, panhandled, or hustled. Some took food out of dumpsters or ate in soup kitchens. Others sold bottles and cans to recycling centers for a little cash.

PUBLIC ASSISTANCE

People with certain forms of mental disorders are eligible for government support in the form of Supplemental Security Income (SSI). But applying for SSI is a long, complicated, and frustrating process involving a great deal of documentation and multiple denials, often taking months or years before applications are approved. Total and permanent disability is the government's standard for approving a person for SSI.

Some of the most disorganized people in this book were never able to navigate the process precisely because they were so disorganized. Others were deemed technically ineligible for one reason or another, sometimes because they could not get a doctor to advocate for them, at other times because they didn't have access to the requisite paperwork. Yet some were able to obtain some form of public assistance and housing; they had usually been vigorously assisted by social workers who were dedicated

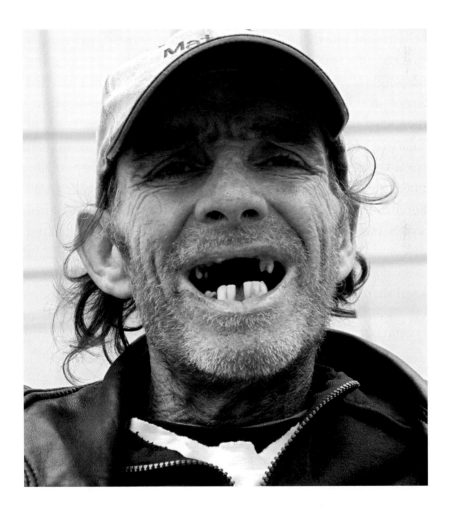

to helping them. These were the lucky ones. They illustrate what is possible with concrete human assistance.

OBSTACLES TO GETTING AND KEEPING A JOB

Living outside creates serious obstacles to getting and keeping a job, making it difficult to escape from the homeless condition. Homelessness makes it tough to get or stay clean for a job interview because people are constantly out in the elements, getting rained and blown on, and absorbing the exhaust, grime, and dirt of the street. Many men told me with embarrassment that although they were afraid their bodies and clothes smelled, they found it almost impossible to clean up because they didn't have easy access to showers and had no clean clothes.

Even if they could get hold of some presentable clothes, they had no place to store them. No matter how diligent they were about their possessions, they frequently lost them or had them stolen. Anything they didn't actually have their hands around, and many things they did, had a habit of "walking away." And even if they did manage to snag a job, they had no place to keep their possessions while they were working. They couldn't very well push their shopping cart through the front door of the business that just hired them and ask the person at the front desk to guard it while they worked.

Further, homeless people lack contact information to give to prospective employers. Without an address or telephone number, a homeless person has no obvious way for a prospective employer to contact him or her, so the employer will simply call the next person on the list, someone who is reachable. Even if a homeless person secures an interview, an admission of home-lessness often prompts the next question—about his or her drug and alcohol history, and after that, his or her criminal history. The shame of opening up about all of this and then being rejected for it is too much for most of these people, especially because they suspect that even if they could get in the front door and actually get the job, they wouldn't be able to do it.

This is not evidence of some neurotic, unrealistic lack of confidence. It reflects a view of themselves that has been well-earned by repeated experience. Because so many of the people in this situation see themselves as failures, they have little trust that they can do anything other than panhandle, hustle, or depend on the government. Even if their external manner is aggressive, demanding, or entitled, this is usually a defensive façade. Most are convinced that they have no right to expect anything from anyone, because they see themselves as such total losers.

It could be argued that not all of these obstacles to regular employment are insurmountable. There are places, though not very accessible, that homeless people can bathe. They could wash themselves in a public bathroom, although this is easier said than done. They could scrape together enough cash to get a clean pair of pants, a shirt, and some decent shoes. And they could get a friend to watch their cart and possessions while they interviewed for a job.

Some of us, no doubt, could pull ourselves out of this cycle—especially if we were smart, had stable and non-abusive early life histories, had someone in our childhoods who loved and believed in us, and particularly if we did okay in school. Some of us could learn the survival skills needed to function in a complicated, highly technical society, especially if we had no addictions, no serious medical or psychiatric problems, and some source of social support. But without these advantages, it is doubtful that most of us would be able to find and keep a job. It is usually the combination and interaction of personal limitations and circumstantial obstacles that defeat people in the end, even if one or the other alone could be surmounted. And luck has a lot to do with this.

PANHANDLING

Even for street-savvy guys, panhandling is tough, unreliable, boring, and poorly paid, requiring a huge amount of patience, tenacity, and a tough outer shell. What people who panhandle hate most about it is the indifference, annoyance, and contempt with which they are regarded. I once spent a morning with someone who panhandled, and I calculated that in the course of a six-hour day, rain or shine, he was passed by 25,000 cars and averaged .06 cent per car, which translated to $2.50 an hour. Whatever one thinks about the ethics of panhandling, it is an inefficient way to make a living. Moreover, anyone who thinks panhandling is easy and people who do it are simply lazy should try it for a few hours in the winter, or even the summer, and see whether they still think so.

So why do people panhandle? Not because they're lazy. Basically, they do it because they're poor and out of other options. They're functionally unemployable, either because they are caught in the cycle of homelessness and joblessness, or because of their drug use, lack of motivation, psychiatric symptoms, or functional deficits. And although not technically disabled by federal or state standards, many people who panhandle have either been deemed ineligible for public assistance or can't navigate the application process.

REACTIONS TO LIVING ON THE STREET

Most of the people I met during the course of this project had lived on the street for years, enduring various situations, such as sleeping on a heating grate, being hosed down by the city's street cleaning trucks early in the morning, or living in a tent in the hills and being hunted down by police. Many described their difficulty finding public bathrooms and the humiliation of being forced to urinate or defecate between buildings or in the bushes. As one man, who was able to get a room with the help of his social worker, told me, "I'd kill myself if I had to go back to the streets. Once you've been inside, there is no way you can go back out there again."

While most found sleeping on the street intolerable, several told me that they actually preferred it to the housing options available to them. A number of individuals said they lived outside because even the most miserable hotel room cost over $600 a month. Those who were not receiving government support couldn't afford even this. Many others who did receive support ($850/month) did not want to spend it on housing, since this would have left them with almost nothing to pay for any other expenses in their lives. One man preferred to use his SSI money for headphones, watches, and so on; other people preferred to use this money for drugs. Additional reasons people gave for choosing to live outside included the distraction from their inner demons provided by dealing with the constant physical demands of survival, freedom from the social pressures of living with others, a dislike of confinement, a fear of catching others' infections, a fear of being preyed upon by other clients, and simply an attraction to the freedom of the street. Still others were so suspicious and paranoid about others that sleeping close to them stirred up their anxiety and psychotic fears and caused them to choose the street over shelters.

Against All Odds

In the course of this project, there were individuals who, against all odds, extracted themselves from life on the street, drug addiction, crime, and prostitution. Several of the people I met were real success stories. With the right combination of services, they were able to shake their addictions, take their psychiatric medications, get into supportive housing, and transform their lives. One man, who had suffered for 10 years with severe addiction and depression, is now drug-free, living in an apartment, and working part-time. Another man, after fighting severe depression and alcoholism, living on the street, and eating from garbage cans, was ultimately coaxed into a support system, where he is now working as an assistant manager of a homeless kitchen. One woman, after living as a drug-addicted prostitute on the street, was able to make use of a case manager, a drug program, and housing to free herself from drugs and the lifestyle required to support her habit. Another woman, who struggled with bipolar disorder and alternately lived in shelters and on a bus, was finally helped by a case manager to find a subsidized apartment and take psychiatric medications.

Breaking the Cycle
of Social Stigma

The negative views I held of people with mental disorders going into this journey were only slowly dislodged by my experiences. It is disheartening to recognize that these views are so tenacious. Sociological studies show that even when we intellectually know better, we respond to these disorders with fear, anger, scorn, blame, and disparagement. We continue to view homelessness and mental disorders as evidence of some deep personal flaw, proof of some intrinsic badness or guilt, a sign that the person suffering from them has done, thought, or felt something terribly wrong and therefore carries a permanent stain on his or her fundamental humanity.

Not only are these reactions ubiquitous, they are often as destructive as the disorders themselves. They not only wreak havoc with people's self-regard, evoking shame, guilt, self-hatred, and despair, but they also have very tangible and destructive social, economic, and political consequences that intimately affect people's lives. Almost everyone I spoke to carried the scars of this stigma.

The people I met had internalized these attitudes. Their predominant characterization of themselves was, "I'm a fuck-up!" Even though some recognized that the deck had been stacked against them from early in their lives, this in no way made them less self-forgiving. What they dwelt on most were the ways they had sabotaged themselves, disappointed others, and rejected offers of help. As one man put it so eloquently, "If you have a big nose, well, no one can blame you. It's just the way you were born. But if you have no teeth, it's proof that you've fucked up real bad and that you must be nothing but a fuck-up."

While at first blush there may be some evidence to support this kind of self-condemnation, even the most cursory look at the lives of these people reveals that this is only part of the story. For the vast majority of people who were willing to talk with me, the trajectory of self-sabotage was set early in life by their biological vulnerabilities and their wounding childhoods. Their own contribution to messing up their lives, though real, was more an effect for which they deserved understanding than a cause for which they deserved blame.

Beyond the immediate impact of stigma on the individual's self-worth, optimism, sense of efficacy, and motivation, the negative branding associated with mental disorders also has powerful effects at social, economic, and political levels. Reducing people to some "flaw," viewing them as fundamentally different, negates our ability to identify and empathize with them, and leads to a perception that they are somehow less human than the rest of us. When a group of people is viewed as less human, others with more social capital feel entitled to treat them as such. This entitlement to dehumanize, enforced by social power, has almost no limits. The devalued group, particularly if also feared and blamed, as in the case of people with mental disorders, finds itself subject to the most extreme forms of neglect and abuse. People with mental disorders have almost never escaped this fate. Throughout history, millions have been beaten, chained, banished to the countryside, or reduced to living in barns and pigsties. But this is not simply their *history*: this treatment is occurring today, with 200,000 abandoned on the street, and another 250,000 incarcerated in jails and prisons. This is, of course, an understatement of the problem, because an even larger number of mentally ill people are subject to other forms of legally sanctioned discrimination and neglect in almost all spheres of life, most notably in health care, housing, and jobs. The consequences of this can be found in their untreated symptoms and abject poverty.

Ironically, many of the characteristics that make these people seem strange and different from us are not an intrinsic part of their disorders but a result of our social and political decision to keep them impoverished. The features of their poverty (toothlessness, tattered clothes, shopping carts, and other aspects of their lives on the street) in turn make them look stranger and weirder than they would otherwise, which intensifies our reluctance to share our resources with them. And the cycle reinforces itself.

And then there is the pervasive sense of hopelessness we have about these people, a belief that there is no intervention that would "get them off the street." This contributes to our tendency to "vote against them" at the ballot box, to deny them the resources they need. It is common to hear legislators justifying their reluctance to spend money on services for the mentally ill by arguing that allocating funds for this purpose would be like "throwing money down a rathole"; that is, it would have no real effect. My conclusion from the work I've done in the hospital and on the street has always confirmed my conviction that most people, no matter how dramatic their presentation, can be helped, and that the gap between what we know can help these people and what we are actually doing as a society to help is enormous. The hopelessness with which we approach this problem has become a self-fulfilling prophecy.

Perhaps this cycle would be less tenacious if it were not reinforced by another that involves our tendency to avoid any meaningful contact with these people. Our avoidance, the ways we remain deaf to their stories and blind to their faces, has the effect of nailing in and reinforcing our conviction that they are fundamentally different from us, because we never really give ourselves the chance to develop another perspective. We don't see that beneath their symptoms and rags are people struggling in their own ways with intense feelings and needs, most of which are similar to our own. And this, in turn, contributes to our tendency to shun them, because they continue to seem so foreign, different, and strange. One of the reasons I wrote this book was to contribute to making these people known as human beings, thus reducing this pernicious cycle of social stigma. Perhaps the reader, on seeing their faces and listening to their stories, will come to regard them with a new perspective. Perhaps he or she will then vote differently at the ballot box when services for mentally ill homeless people are on the budgetary chopping block. Perhaps then these people will finally have a chance in life.

IMAGES

&

STORIES

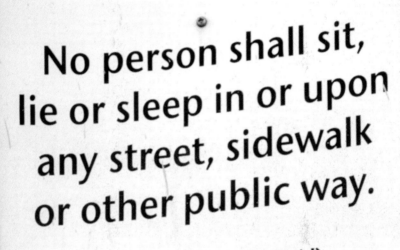

No person shall sit, lie or sleep in or upon any street, sidewalk or other public way.

L.A.M.C. Sec. 41.18 (d)
Violators are subject to prosecution

POSTED BY PROPERTY OWNER

"I USED TO LIVE IN A HOME. NOW I LIVE IN A CARDBOARD BOX." —MARY

I almost passed without noticing her, so small and still was she, sitting against the large, grey, bleak wall of the San Francisco Public Library. She seemed to be gazing at her hands, which were loosely folded in her lap. I walked back and kneeled in front of her. I told her I thought her face was beautiful and asked if I could take her photograph for this book. She smiled sadly and told me she had once been very beautiful, but that was a long time ago.

I was totally absorbed. Was it by her gentleness or her sadness or some vision of what she had lost?

She had once lived with a man who had hurt her, and she had used drugs to soothe herself. Then she lost everything.

As she told me how her life had collapsed, she began to weep. I couldn't bear to photograph her at that moment.

"THE ANGELS OF SUFFERING ARE SCREECHING AT ME!"

—DAVID

"Can't you see them? They're shooting things into my brain! They won't stop torturing me! Even in my room they don't leave me alone!"

David approached me when I was about to cross the street. Perhaps he noticed my camera and thought I was one of his tormentors, or perhaps he hoped that I knew them and could intervene on his behalf.

My first instinct was to pretend I hadn't heard him. I didn't really know what to say. In the hospital, I care for many people who say strange things. I'm not usually lost for a response, perhaps because I have some measure of control and power there. On the street, I am on *their* turf, where I feel professionally naked and where similar encounters often leave me wordless.

Before I could recover myself, he began talking volubly, with a painful intensity. His drift was difficult to follow, and it was not easy to interrupt him. When I tried, however gently, he became more agitated. At some point, not knowing what else to do, I put my hand on his arm, which seemed to calm him. There was something in his eyes that betrayed as much longing for closeness as fear of it.

He told me that he was born in Oregon to parents who separated when he was 7. He spent a confusing childhood being passed back and forth between them. At 13, he was sent to a

home for juveniles, from which he regularly escaped—only to be returned each time by the police.

Defined as an adult on his 18th birthday, he was allowed to leave the facility. He had nowhere to go, so he lived on the streets in various cities. During his 20s, he became increasingly convinced that extraterrestrial creatures were shooting particles into his brain.

Currently, he lives in San Francisco, is supported by social welfare, and lives in one of the city's transient hotels. To my surprise, he agreed to let me visit him there.

His room was disheveled. In his toilet was a can of shaving cream, some of which was smeared on the mirror. He refused to allow anyone to help him clean because he didn't want strangers in his room, touching his things.

He passes his days walking around the city trying to duck the cameras he is convinced are tracking him. At times he becomes so delusional and confused that he can no longer take care of himself. When things reach this point, he is hospitalized and given medication, but as soon as he leaves the hospital, he dumps his pills down the toilet, fearing they will poison his brain. And the cycle begins again.

"IS THAT ALL YOU COULD GET ME?" —Daniel

I passed him sitting against a Walgreens drug store in the financial district, with a cigarette in his mouth. He barely responded to me other than to say that he panhandled during the day and slept in doorways at night. He also told me that he had been placed many times in the psychiatric ward of the city hospital.

He asked me to buy him a bowl of chili. When I did so and handed it to him, he looked up at me and scowled, *"Is that all you could get me?"*

I bought him another portion, which seemed to satisfy him.

"HE NEEDS TO SEE I'VE DONE MY PENANCE."

— BARBARA

"The first time I was in prison was for armed robbery when I was 15. I was completely strung out on heroin. I had rounded up two guys to help me hold up a pharmacy. The pharmacist didn't hand over the drugs right away so I aimed the gun just over his head and pulled the trigger. I didn't hit him. The other guys got caught and ratted on me. I was tried in adult court and got five years to life because I was the shooter. I was in prison for 14 months but got out on a technicality.

"I don't know when I was actually born. My mother told me 1943, but my birth certificate says 1949. My mother and father were already separated. My brother and sister and I all had different fathers. When I was two or three, my father kidnapped me and moved me around from one state to another so no one could find us. We were discovered two years later, and I was returned to my mother. I was told later that there was some suspicion that he had molested me.

"My mother had been a wild bar girl during the war. She used to tell me stories that sounded so enticing. I was her biggest fan. I followed in her footsteps because I wanted to be a character in one of her dramas. Also, I guess it was a way of staying close to her in my mind. To this day, I don't know which stories are hers and which are mine.

"When I was a teenager, I hopped freight trains and rode the rails all around the country. And then I got into crack and then into armed robberies. I was shot several times in the stomach

and the legs, usually by the police. I got away with 43 burglaries, but during the 44th, I was caught and put in prison for three years.

"I met my husband when I was 25. We lived together on and off for 23 years. We had a son together. When I was delivering in the hospital, my son got stuck in the birth canal waiting for the doctor to come, and was born deaf. He wouldn't have been born at all if I hadn't grabbed the nurse by the collar and shouted at her, 'This baby's gonna die if you don't get it out!' He needed a lot of special help as a kid.

"When I was 48, my husband locked himself in the bathroom to fix and died of a heroin overdose. At the time, I had been gone for three days, strung out on crack and turning tricks to feed my habit and pay the rent. I don't know how long it took for my son to get worried enough to start banging on the door, but he couldn't get my husband to open it.

"I can't seem to forgive myself, you know, for doing something so stupid as smoking that glass prick of crack and not being there when my husband needed me and forcing my son to find him. After that, my life stopped. I lost my mind. At first I couldn't even come up with a desire to eat. I got so skinny I had to walk into a room twice to cast a shadow. I had no desire to do anything but smoke crack and use heroin because there was the chance that I might take something that wasn't survivable.

"And I was having a hard time making it home for my son, and I was sleeping in the street more and more. My son could see me from the window while I was out in the street, working. To this day, I see his face looking out the window at me, wanting me to come in. I don't know why I didn't come in for him. When he was 12, he was taken away from me and put into the foster care system. I lost track of him for years. I can't really forgive myself for making him go through all of that.

"After my son was taken, I lived out of a shopping cart. I didn't feel I had the right to come in. I wasn't really living because I didn't really want to.

"When a woman is homeless, no matter how clean she is about her person, and I was pretty clean, people can tell. I'd stop and take a whore's bath every day. I'd go to the parking garage and

would wash my body and feet in the bathroom, then use the hand drier and stuff. I kept myself in clothes that were moderately commercial, you know, and I still had my teeth at that time, but you can't really hide it when you're homeless, using, and turning tricks. And the longer I stayed strung out, the worse I looked, so it became harder and harder to make money on the street, and it took longer and longer to make. It's a story I don't like to really talk about because it took me a long time to come back from that, and I'm still coming back from it.

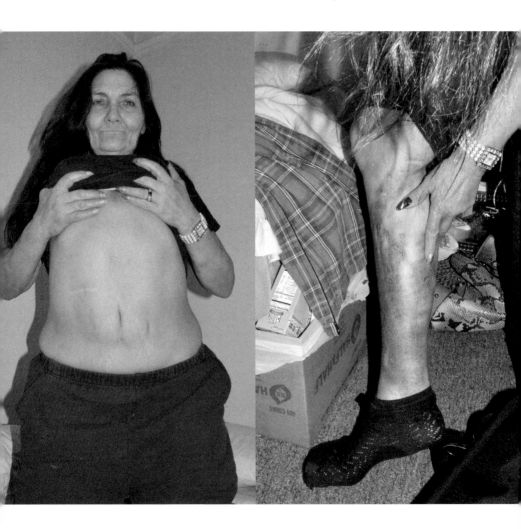

"Once, I was hospitalized on a psychiatric unit for a drug over-dose, and because I was such a mess and because I was always putting myself in dangerous situations. The doctor told me I had manic depression. When I'd get depressed, I wouldn't want to live. When I got manic, I became hyper, I couldn't concentrate, couldn't live in my own skin, did crazy things.

"It was a cop who saved my life. He found me squatting in an alley with a needle in my arm. He took me to the methadone program at San Francisco General Hospital. 'This is your chance,' he told me. 'The next time, you're going to jail.' I started taking methadone and got into a case management program. My social worker helped me get meds for my manic depression, got me onto welfare, and helped me get a room. I've been clean now for five years. I eat one meal a day and live on $20 a week. Primarily, I live on cereal and maybe a sweet potato and a vegetable.

"Living in this building with so many addicts and ex-addicts is a challenge. It's hard to keep my things safe here. Either they're stolen by other clients, by the staff who have a key to my room, or by the fire department because all the papers I have here supposedly creates a fire hazard.

"One of the toughest things about my life right now is not hav-ing any teeth. When I was living on the street, I lost them all to infection. I finally got Medicaid to pay for fake ones four years ago, but they were run over by a car, only months after I had got-ten them. I was getting out of a bus when someone accidentally pushed me off the last step onto the street. My jaw hit the pave-ment, and out jumped my teeth into the path of an oncoming car. The last I saw of them they were little white things stuck into the car's tire, rolling down the street. I have to wait another year before I can get them replaced because Medicaid will only *pay for teeth once every five years. It's not easy to eat. I chew my food the best I can and then swallow the rest whole.*

"But the worst is that I hate the way I look. I don't like smiling and I don't feel like flirting. I used to be pretty, but now when I look at myself in the mirror, I see a fat, toothless old woman.

"I still miss my husband incredibly. I still talk to him in my mind. It's been 10 years and I know it's time for me to move on, but I just can't seem to do it. I don't feel like I really deserve to bring anyone else into my life for some reason, which makes it impossible to let anyone get close to me. It's as though I'm always waiting for something, like the record button is stuck on hold.

"Maybe if my son accepted me, my life would change. I haven't seen him since he was 12. He's 20 now and in college somewhere. I lost the only photo I had of him, when I was living on the streets. I don't have his address, but I send him any extra money I have through someone who knows how to reach him. I don't think he's at the point where he really wants to see me yet. And I guess I'm afraid to see him. I've suggested meeting him a couple of times, but it never actually happened. Either he didn't make it or I didn't make it. I just want him to know I'm there for him. He needs to see I've done my penance."

I went to see Barbara in her hotel room a year after our initial conversations. She had been "graduated" from her case management program because she had been able to stabilize her life (i.e., she had a roof over her head and was no longer using drugs). She was still unable to figure out how to find her son's new contact information but told me she probably wouldn't write to him anyway, fearing he would tell her that he wanted nothing to do with her. At this point, she became tearful.

At the time of this last conversation, it was late December, and her room was so cold that both of us had to keep our winter coats on. She told me that despite four written complaints, she hadn't been able to get the hotel management to fix her radiator since it had broken down the previous winter.

When we approached the hotel manager, he could find "only" one complaint that Barbara had written eight months earlier and assumed the problem had been fixed. By the time I left, he had found an electric heater to tide her over "temporarily," although this, he informed us, was in violation of the fire code. Was he implying that he was doing Barbara a favor she should be grateful for?

I was struck by Barbara's powerlessness to get something so simple, yet so essential, addressed. Being "graduated" from her program did her no favors, as she still obviously needed the support and advocacy that it had provided her. It was just one of the many examples I encountered of health care rationing, in which one client, having become barely stable, gets pushed off the rolls in order to make way for another client who is marginally more impaired and in need of service.

A few months following my last contact with Barbara, I attempted to call her. I was told she was dead, killed by a rapidly metastasizing cancer. I never expected her to die in this way. A

drug overdose after a relapse, hypothermia from exposure, perhaps infection—but not cancer.

Notwithstanding the brevity of our friendship, her death has
left a noticeable hole in my heart.

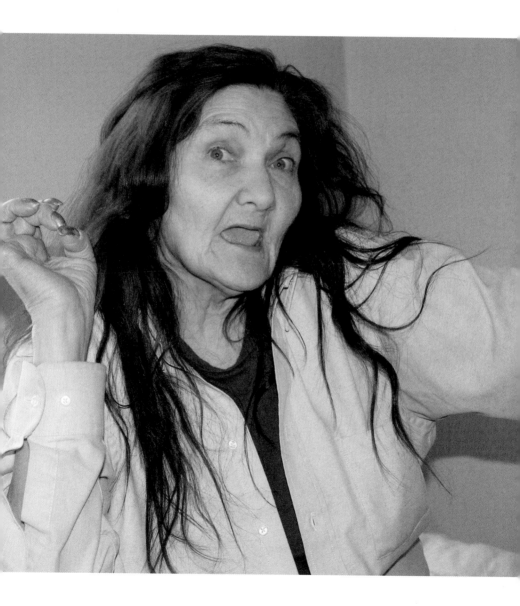

THE CHESS GAME

I played three games of chess with a man on Market Street. There were 10 other games going on simultaneously. For the price of $2, a chess board could be rented, and $5 bets placed.

My opponent was demented. He asked me what my name was after every other move and kept shouting out the date of his birth. Every few minutes, someone would irritably threaten to throw him into the traffic if he didn't "shut his fuckin' mouth." But nothing could stop the man's relentless yelling.

Every time he reached for his chess piece, his hand shook so violently that it was impossible to tell which he intended to move. Not until he had actually grasped the piece did it become clear.

In each of three games against him, I didn't last more than 12 moves. I lost $15 in a quarter of an hour.

MAN EXAMINING HIS SOCK

I sat beside him for over an hour. He seemed completely unaware of my presence, so intently was he examining his sock. When I returned two hours later, he was sitting in the same spot, still gazing at it.

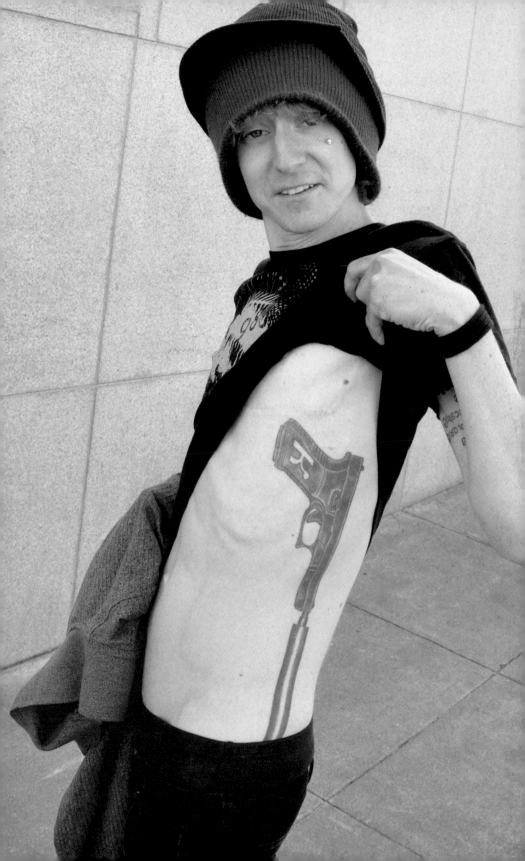

"THE WORLD ENDED IN 1967, AND THERE'S NO PLACE TO GO." —MAN WITH HIS BICYCLE

I had been watching this man push his bike around the financial district on a sultry day. The bike was loaded with all his possessions. Its rear tire was flat. He sat down to drink, at which point I approached him. During the course of a short, awkward conversation, I asked him about his flat tire.

"Yea, my tire's flat. So what?"

"Wouldn't it be easier for you to push your bike if it weren't?" I suggested.

"What difference would it make? The world ended in 1967, and there's no place to go anyway," he said irritably, as though any jerk could have seen that. He waved me away.

As I turned to leave, he looked up at the sky and said philosophically, *"If it's raining, you can't fix the roof, and if it's not raining, you don't have to fix the roof."*

I met him again six months later. He looked thinner and more haggard.

"There's a guy in the city who flies around. 'Cause, you know, when you buzz a place, or how many places have you buzzed?" *"I've never buzzed anyplace."*

"Well, I used to blow a helicopter."
"You used to what?"
"Well, a helicopter!"

"You flew a helicopter?"
"No, I fly a helicopter! If I had a helicopter, I'd fly out of here."

"Where would you go?"
"Out of here!"

"Yea, but do you know where you'd go?"
"I'd just fly out of here! Anywhere! 'Cause there's no airport."

I had to keep reminding myself that he was the "crazy" one, not I.

WOMAN WITH HER SLEEPING BAG —ALEXANDRA

I saw a blue sleeping bag floating down the street. I followed it for a few minutes and watched two hands emerge and dig into a trash can, pulling out and drinking a discarded, half-finished cup of coffee. I maneuvered myself in front of the enshrouded figure and asked if she wanted to go for coffee with me. She came but was hard to engage in conversation. She told me in a flat Italian accent that her name was Alexandra, that she had come to San Francisco from Italy the previous year on vacation but couldn't remember exactly where in that country she'd come from. There was almost nothing else she could recall, except that she'd had some kind of fall but couldn't remember where it had happened or whether she had lost consciousness.

She said that she slept on the street and ate what people threw away. I asked her whether she got cold at night and whether there was anything I could do for her. She responded no and no. She seemed totally unperturbed about her situation, including her complete loss of recall. In fact, she said that she didn't really want to remember anything.

She politely thanked me for the coffee and said she needed to be on her way. I saw her a few hours later changing her shirt in the middle of the square, totally unaware that people were staring at her.

"I'M GONNA DIE SOONER OR LATER. I DON'T REALLY CARE WHEN. I'M TOO SAD." —TATANKA LUTA

"They call me Tatanka Luta, Alma Red Bull. I'm a Sioux warrior. I'm a very strong man. I grew up in South Dakota on a reservation, and I been stuck here since 2000. Back home, my daughter and wife died in a head-on collision."

He was crouching against a store window on Market Street when I approached him. I asked him how long ago it had happened.

"Nineteen eighty-three. My daughter, Lalita, was only three years old. Goddamn fuckin' Navajo drinking. They were going up the hill in a car, and a truck smashed into them. I was at work in the Navajo mines when it happened. It's karma. My dad got run over by a semitruck when I was three. A few years later, my mom was killed by a guy who ran into her with his car when she was crossing the street. So my whole family was totally wiped out. My whole life was wiped out.

"After my wife and daughter died, I stopped working. I stopped living. Fuck everything! I had a stereo, clothes, TV, food in the refrigerator. I said fuck it, man, I'm outta here. I took my truck and I wrecked it around and a pole. People didn't like me because I was mad, I was so mad. But you can't never be angry at God. Because things happen for a reason. I pray, I just pray, man. People try to talk to me, but I don't want to pay attention. All they say, 'We're very sorry it happened.'

"I never drank before they were killed. Now, I have to keep drinkin'. It calms my soul.

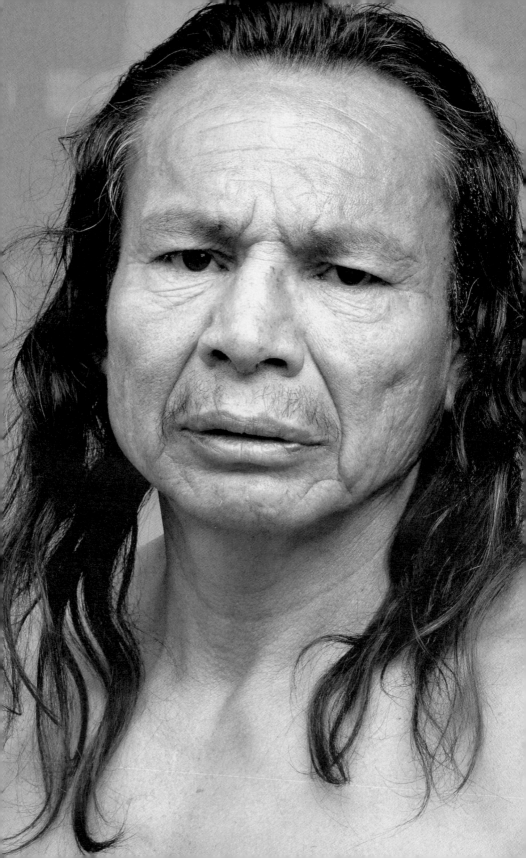

"I'm gonna die sooner or later. I don't really care when. I'm too sad. All I do is walk around by myself, try to be happy, that's all. Walk around, walk around. All night long I walk around the city. In the rain, I walk around, too. I always walk all over the place, man. I go to Two Hills to pray. I sleep in the bushes near the movie theater around here. There's more cover than on the streets. I just want to stay alone because I'm too sad. No home, no daughter, no wife. I'm still so angry, man!"

"I WAS FOUR YEARS ON DEATH ROW." —MAN WITH HIS DOG

I was walking along Haight Street in San Francisco when I saw a man with a pitbull.

"Can I take a picture of your dog?" I asked.
"Go ahead. I don't give a fuck!" he answered in a Southern drawl.

"Will he bite me if I pet him?"
"Ask him. I don't know. Sometime he do and sometime he don't. When his eyes cross, nobody know for sure."

"What's his name?
"Lipshit."

"Lipshit? Where in the world did he get that name?" I asked, laughing.
"His name used to be Nigel. He didn't answer to that. So one day I called him Lipshit. He looked up, so that's his name now. He's a hump doggin' dude," he said proudly. *"The other day, he jumped up and bit me right on my dick. Dirty Ernie. Yesterday he was on top my arm. A cop who was writin' me a ticket for drinkin' said, 'What's that dog doin'?' I said, 'He's humpin' my arm. Whatta ya think he's doin'?'"*

"How did you learn to tell such colorful stories?"
"I was four years on death row. I had a lotta time to practice."
All humor was gone in an instant.

"How did you come to be on death row?"
"I caught a guy molestin' my daughter. I blew him in half with a shotgun. The state was gonna gas me, but at the last minute I got

"MY TWO DAUGHTERS WERE BLOWN TO BITS BY SUICIDE BOMBERS IN IRAQ." —HEIDI

I met Heidi at the Ferry Building in San Francisco. She was sitting alone on a concrete wall, holding onto a cart filled with her possessions. She related her story in a pressured, rambling, jerky manner, speaking almost inaudibly at times. I frequently had to ask her to repeat herself and often wondered whether I had missed the connection between parts of what she was saying. I have edited her narrative for the sake of coherence, but the language is hers and I haven't added anything of substance.

"I had three kids. Two were girls. Laura went into the army when she was 19 and was sent to Iraq. One year later, she was blown up by a little girl with explosives attached to her. All I have left of Laura is a flag and her rusty dog tags. There was nothing left to bury.

"I pleaded with my second daughter, Nina, to stay out of the army, but she enlisted anyway as soon as she was 18 in order to 'kick some fuckin' ass over in Iraq.' She went to revenge her sister, but as soon as she got there, she was killed by a roadside bomb. And now I have no more daughters—only a 14-year-old son who keeps telling me that he's going to go into the army 'to bring Nina and Laura home.' He's living in Nebraska with his father.

"My mother told me that I started drinking when I was a year old. My dad took care of me during the day while she worked. He put whiskey in my bottle to keep me quiet. When I was in

elementary school, my teacher discovered whiskey mixed with my milk. She took it away, and I went into DTs.

"My father left my mom and me when I was five. He married someone else and never gave a penny to us. I lived with my mom until I was about 11 and then started running away because my stepfather was molesting me. I started skipping school and not coming home at night. A judge took me away from my mom because she couldn't control me. I lived in foster homes and shelters and sometimes with my grandmother. When I was 13, I was put into juvenile homes. I was in the system for two years. It wasn't right that I should do time for being hurt by my stepfather.

"I got married when I was 15. He was 23. I managed not to get pregnant until I was 18. He kept beating me up. One day, when I was pregnant with twins, he went crazy, punched me to the

floor and kicked my face with his steel-toe boots. He broke my jaw and I lost all my teeth on the right side of my mouth. I had to have my jaw wired for months. The twins died. Then one day, I put a hard ball in a sock and beat the living shit out of him. That man never laid hands on me again. I was 21 when I got away from him.

"I've been drinking on and off for years, and now I have a bad crack habit. I've had leukemia for a long time. I don't live in a shelter because I don't want to be packed into a room with five other people. My leukemia has hurt my immune system, and God knows what diseases are running around the shelters. It's safer for me to live on the streets. I sleep near the second column under the Bay Bridge with my boyfriend, Jeff, when he's around.

"I've been going with Jeff for eight years. But he uses speed, and I never know when he'll be here and when he won't. I spend most of my time waiting for him to show up. After six hours, I go back to the Bay Bridge, pissed off, disappointed, and wondering where in the world he is and when I'm going to see him again.

"I'm pregnant now, in my first trimester. Jeff hasn't fucked me in months. My sexuality is color-coded. When I'm in a red mood, I want to be fucked long and hard. When I'm in a yellow mood, I want it soft. When I'm in a black mood, I want it fast, bang, bang, bang, and then exit. It's the way I get my anger out."

On one occasion, Heidi told me that she had missed several of her prenatal appointments at the hospital. Though I had my doubts about her "pregnancy," I urged her to keep her next appointment and told her that I'd accompany her if she wished. She agreed, but our intention was almost thwarted by not knowing what to do with her cart and its possessions. We couldn't take it on the bus, we couldn't wheel it five miles to the hospital, we couldn't find a safe place to store it, we couldn't simply leave it unattended on the street, and we couldn't initially find anyone to guard it for the afternoon.

Many physicians, including me at times, fail to recognize that patients can't get to the hospital for their appointments unless they figure out a solution to this problem. This, like so many other problems faced by homeless people, tends to be invisible from the vantage point of a traditional office setting. And on that day with Heidi, notwithstanding all my training and experience, and all the resources in the city at my disposal, I could not come up with a way of dealing with Heidi's cart, short of guarding it myself while she went to her appointment. Just as I was about to suggest this, one of her acquaintances appeared; this person was willing, for a few dollars, to look after her cart. Gratefully, we got on the next bus and rode to the hospital, only to discover that the doctor had been called away on an emergency and the clinic was closed. Back we went to retrieve her cart three hours later.

One of the last times I saw Heidi, I almost failed to recognize her. She was dressed in leggings, black shorts, and a red blouse, her hair pulled into pigtails. She was wearing lipstick, mascara, and a sweet-smelling perfume. She told me she had been made up by a cosmetics clerk at a nearby store who wanted to help her "get her man back." She had been waiting for Jeff in the hot sun all day, dressed in this outfit. When she finally realized that he wasn't going to show, she crumpled in disappointment and sobbed.

"WELL, I DON'T KNOW WHAT ROCK BOTTOM IS, IF THIS ISN'T IT. I HAVE NOTHING LEFT!" —RYAN

"I'm on a five-day speed run. I haven't slept for two or three days. I can hardly think straight.

"I have a bad, bad habit. Just the word 'speed' sets me off. It has me so bad. So bad. When I just think about the meth getting into my blood, I start sweating I want it so much. No one can stop me if I have a mind to use. And once I start, I can't stop. It's so hard to get off. I'm too weak. And I can always get it, even when I don't have any money. Dealers give it to me free because I bring them customers, my friends. I call them my friends, but you know what? They're not. The only thing that helps me is pot. It helps my craving for a while. But the craving always comes back.

"People say, 'Well, you haven't hit rock bottom yet.' And I say, 'Well, I don't know what rock bottom is, if this isn't it. I have nothing left!' My friend died from a brain aneurysm he got from speed, man. I see what it can do to you, and I still can't stop. Sometimes I think I'll only stop using when I'm dead.

"You know what? All the services I'm offered, I blow. A program is only going to work for someone who wants it. If you have any kind of ambivalence, it's not going to work. I know this is fucked up, but I need a reason to stop. I need a person in my life. I need something to pull me in a positive direction. But no one's going to save my life. I've got to do it.

"Sex is a big part of it. You could put a wig on a pig, and I'd go after it when I'm on speed. It just makes all your fantasies come true. That's the hardest part to give up. I have all kinds

of sexual fantasies, mostly about older women, incest. I don't want to talk about it. I had a fucked-up childhood, babysitters and shit. Meth makes your body feel so good. Think of the best orgasm you ever had and multiply it times 1,000. When I'm on a run, I want to fuck, fuck, fuck. Even after you come, your body still feels wonderful. I sometimes fuck for 15 hours. I'm a freak when I'm on meth.

"I'm also addicted to women. I gotta have them. That's probably why I did [i.e., initiated into drugs] my girlfriend, Crystal. Her ex-boyfriend did me. I did her. I'm sick, in my head. I put a needle in her arm and got her addicted to meth. That's the worst thing I ever did in my life. She had had some argument with her dad, and she pleaded, 'Give me some.' 'Crystal, no, no!' I said. 'Give me some!' 'No, No!' She kept going on and on. And finally I said, 'Shut your fuckin' mouth. Here.' And I ended up putting it in her. But I never wanted to hurt her—never, never. She was my first love. I was truly in love with her for three years. And you know what makes it even worse? The first 18 months we were together, she helped me stay clean and sober, and this is how I paid her back!

"I used to be a real scumbag. I was stealing cars as soon as I learned to drive. I'd take the coat off your back. If you let me into your house, I'd steal your suit. I've burned the hand. But that was in the past—six years ago.

"I'm not going to lie. For a time I was doing a lot of shoplifting, but I don't do it anymore. I haven't stole. I don't do shady or underhanded shit anymore. I've been in prison twice either for selling drugs or violating my parole. Prison's a blessing in disguise. It's sad, but it's the only thing that gets me off meth. In reality, you can do just as much drugs inside as you can outside, but when I'm inside, I don't do it 'cause I don't want to get caught. But prison only takes me so far 'cause I start using again the day I get out. And I can see how easy it is to get into the prison lifestyle, 'cause you don't have to take responsibility for anything. All your food, all your clothing, everything is given to you. It's easy. You know what's hard? Keeping a job, feeding your family. That is hard as fuck!

"My dad was strung out on China White [a form of heroin] for years when I was a kid. He'd make up reasons to beat the shit out of my mother and me. When he didn't have a drink, he got worse. My mother used to run to a battered women's shelter and take me with her. Then my parents split, and when I was a teen-ager I lived in group homes. But I had a hard time there, and I got hospitalized on psych units a few times. Every time I went in, they'd give me a new med. One time I was on 13 different meds: Haldol, Mellaril, lithium, Tegretol. I was like a zombie. I can't tell you what helped and what didn't because I was on so many at one time. I know I need meds. I know I'm manic-depressive.

"I'm gonna make it out. I already know it—just like my dad did, when he found God. He's totally changed. He really apologized to me. We're trying to patch things up between us. I know I'm gonna make it. The Lord's on my side. I just need to quit. I just need some kind of medication that blocks the speed. I just need a person in my life. Maybe if I have kids, it will straighten me out. I'm gonna get out of this."

Ryan talked nonstop for an hour, barely pausing to catch his breath. His words tumbled out with speed and intensity. There was something incredibly sweet and naïve about him, a totally lost little boy.

"SOMETIMES I GET TIRED OF HAVING A ROOF OVER MY HEAD." —LINDA

"My name is Linda. I'm living outside the bus terminal. My buddy and I take turns sleeping. I sleep with one eye open because my entire net worth is in this cart. But I'm not really a down-and-out tramp. I get SSI. Every once in a while, when I get tired of living on the streets, shit, I just give up and go live in a cheap hotel.

"But those places are depressing. They throw you in one of those tiny rooms and make you fend for yourself with the crazies and the dopers. After a while, I get sick of all of it. I get tired of having a roof over my head. Sometimes, even when it's winter, I have to get out. I can't take it no more in my room—too depressing. All I was doing was staring at the four walls listening to my nutty neighbors going off. What kind of fun is that? So I decide to hit the streets and be happy instead of being in a room with a bunch of crazies nearby and be miserable. This is more freedom to me, pushing this cart and having a little money to last as long as it does.

"Also there's the rent. I been hearing on the radio they want to cut my $960 SSI check. How much more can they cut? I can't afford rent as it is now. Hell, man, the cheapest hotel room is $700 a month. So after you pay your rent, what are you going to have left over for yourself? Same reason I don't buy gloves. It's cold out, but I'm not goin' to waste my money on gloves. You know what I'm saying? If I spent money on rent and gloves, I couldn't afford something like these gangster headphones and this watch. This watch makes me happy every time I look at it. It kind of reminds me that I'm not a total failure, else I wouldn't have it.

"To me, I have money today, I better spend it, because tomorrow I may not be here, you know what I'm sayin'? I don't know, man, I might get mugged, might get hit by a car. I've always lived day to day ever since I can remember.

"I had a hard life growing up in Chicago. My parents supposedly broke my arm and burned my feet in the fire when I was a kid. Family services took me away from them when I was five or something. I wish I could remember all that. I don't even know *who the hell they were. I been through so many foster parents, more than 10, you know, so to be honest with you, I can't remember what my real parents looked like.*

"I was a problem child. I couldn't concentrate in school. I was always throwing fits and acting up. Nobody seemed to know what the problem was. These foster parents always said they didn't know how to handle me. I don't know what you call it in the foster care business. Undesirable? So I ended being raised up in group homes and institutions.

"After I got out of school, I could never hold down a job for too long, and that's how I got to living on the streets. Then I started thinking crazy shit that I couldn't get out of my mind. Once I went to Safeway and told them I had a bomb in my suitcase, and they called the police. I knew I didn't have a bomb, but I just wanted to get off the streets, man. You know. I waited for the police and everything. They gave me 16 months for that.

"Sometimes I break windows or get so mad I get out of control. Whenever there is too much pressure, that's what happens. I haven't done that in a long time 'cause I learned my lesson. You go crazy on the streets and then, when you're taken to jail, they fuckin' torture you and kick the shit out of you. I'm talkin' about the guards. They got worse torture in jail than in the so-called torture camps that Uncle Sam has, man. They beat the shit out of me in jail. I'm still hurtin' from that beating. You see my thumb? It's still broken from what the guards did to it. That's how it got fucked up. All because I went off, and wasn't getting the right psychiatric help and medicine. Jail is no place for someone with mental problems. They don't give a fuck.

"The mental health system never helped me either. They said I was paranoid schizophrenic. Once I was hospitalized in the psychiatric unit, the doctor gave me medicine. I call it dope. It fucks your dick up, man. You can't get your jollies off when you're on that crap. The doctor didn't even tell me what it was going to do to me. They don't tell you shit no more, man. They just give you that crap, and that's it. I went to beat my meat, you know, do my thing, and nothing came out. 'What the hell?' I said. 'I'm not taking this!'

"When I got out of the hospital, I got a social worker, but he gave up on me because I didn't go to his damn program. It reminded me too much of the group homes I had been cooped up in when I was a kid. When you get out, you tell yourself, 'I can do what I want now. I don't have to go to these places.'

"I'm still tryin' to figure out what I'm supposed to have learned from my life and all. Mostly I try to work it out by myself, because there's no one I'm really close to. I'm what you call a loner—not because I want to be. Because that's the way I was raised. When you ain't learned how to love, when you ain't learned how to be close to somebody, basically you're cooked. If you had parents that were breaking your arms, putting your feet in the fire, there's not much you're going to learn. 'Cept for don't get too close to people. You never know what they're going to do.

"I've always been shy anyway. It's probably why I don't have AIDS. I never had a relationship. No sex, no diseases. Worked out good, but then again, that loneliness can kill you, too. When I get too lonely, which is all the time, I listen to music.

Can't live without it. Every time I get homeless, I always got some music with me. That's my medicine, you know.

"Sometimes the music makes me sad, but I haven't cried in a long time. The last time, I was sitting in a hotel, thinking about my mother—or at least tryin' to remember what she looked like. Usually everybody remembers what their parents were like. I don't. I was always different. I'm a transgender. I don't understand why. I was just born that way, wanting to put on a dress. But I'm not getting my dick cut off. I play both worlds."

As I was packing up my camera, I asked him how he chose to call himself Linda. "It was my mother's name," he replied. "At least I know that about her."

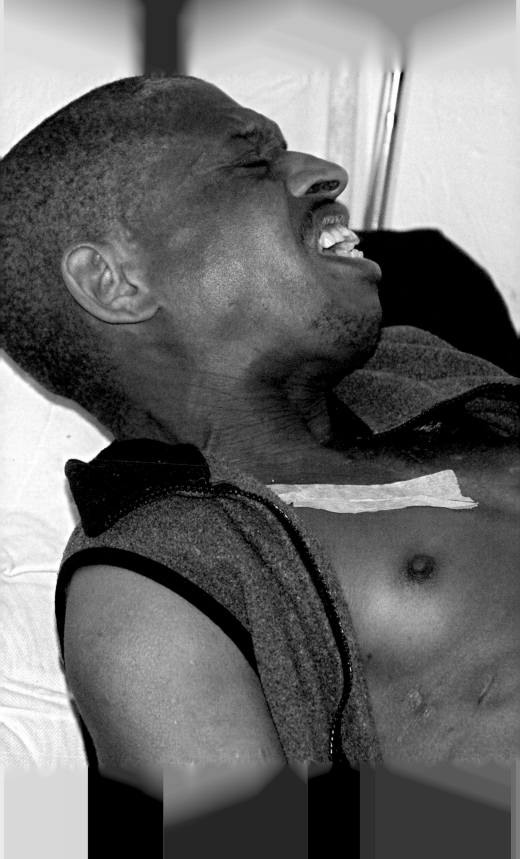

"I'VE TRADED MY PAIN MEDICATION AWAY FOR CRACK."

—Gregg

"I've had sickle cell anemia since I was a boy. I've had hundreds of sickle cell crises since then. They're incredibly painful. They've destroyed the bone in my leg and blinded me in one eye. Sometimes I don't have my pain medication when I need it 'cause I've traded it away for crack."

I met Gregg at a point when he was using crack and other drugs despite having recently obtained housing. He was being seen weekly by a social worker, who helped him with the concrete problems in his life. Crack often precipitated his sickle cell crises. He had an extreme and contorted limp, requiring that he use a cane to walk.

A few months after I met him, he was drawn into an altercation with someone who called him a "nigger" and then attacked him. Gregg struck back with his cane in self-defense. Apprehended by the police, who didn't believe his side of the story, Gregg was sentenced to house arrest for three months and monitored with an electronic collar attached to his ankle. He was also required to attend a drug treatment program and to undergo random drug screens. It was only at this point that he stopped using drugs, whereupon the frequency of his sickle cell crises decreased substantially.

Gregg's early life had been complicated. After he was diagnosed with sickle cell anemia as a boy, his father left the family. His mother, soon after, developed a relationship with a married man who supported her and her six children while he continued to live with his wife. One day when Gregg was an adolescent, he walked in on his mother smoking crack with some of her friends. He thought, "Man, that looks great," and with the encouragement of his older brother, he began using it himself. Over time, he developed a network of friends with whom he smoked, stole, and fought to support his habit.

Gregg's life is a testimony to the compulsive power of crack. When he was stoned, he maintained a cheerful, optimistic, charming bravado that hid his discouragement and sense of defeat. When he didn't have crack, he became a totally different person—desperate and unreachable. From his early 20s, crack had sabotaged his ability to work; drove him into the streets, where he lived for years; destroyed important relationships; led to multiple incarcerations; and regularly provoked extremely painful sickle cell crises.

These crises destroyed the bone in his leg and required the surgical removal of his left eye, but even this and the intense pain of his crises couldn't compete with his addiction. When the pain became too severe, he'd call an ambulance and be taken to the city hospital's emergency room, where he'd be given a small quantity of pain medication to get him through the episode. After several days, he'd feel better, go out to the street, hustle for money and drugs, and start the cycle all over again.

I found myself in an internal struggle, blaming Gregg for some of the misery of his life on the one hand, and recognizing how totally out of control he was on the other. The power of his addiction and his inability to resist it, despite the fact that it was eating away at his body and slowly killing him, took my breath away.

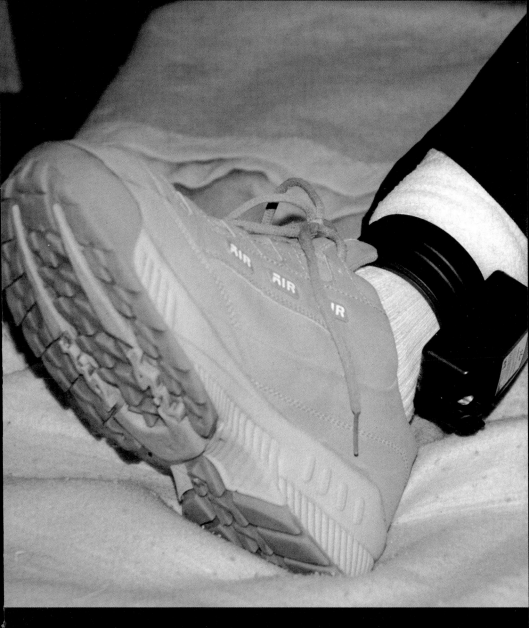

"I'M SURE MY MOM DIDN'T WANT TO GIVE ME AWAY."

—MAN WITH HIS DAFFY TIE

"I'm letting them know that their pyramid scheme is bullshit, because the human condition won't allow it. Thanks, asshole. Whoever was behind me, thank you, I'll clean up your dog shit now. Well, somebody's got to do it."

I heard Rick before I saw him, talking truculently to himself and to everyone who passed. People stepped around him on the path. He eventually came over to where I was sitting and began talking angrily about "assholes, motherfuckers from foreign countries who are trying to steal everything we have." He was pressured and enraged during most of our conversation, and I was able to interrupt him only with the greatest care and deference.

He told me that he had been living on the street for years, had been incarcerated several times for drug possession, had passed through various drug treatment programs, and was thrown out of the last one two years earlier for refusing to take a urine test.

When he began talking about his parents, he began to cry. *"I miss my mother, man. See, she had me from somebody I never met. My mother, she had to give me away to the court when I was 14. I got in trouble with the authorities. Then it was group homes, state raised, ward of the court. I'm sure my mom didn't want to give me away. It was just she couldn't handle me. I don't blame her. I don't hate her. I'm not mad at her. She didn't know any better. She had a hard life, man. She's been duped by her own life. It causes her pain to see me, so I keep away. I'm going to get a truck and live in the mountains like my father did."*

"I FELL FROM THE EMPIRE STATE BUILDING TO THE CURB."

— BRIDGETT

"I met my husband when I was 20. He was dealing and using cocaine. Everyone wanted to talk to him, and I thought that he was very impressive. We lived in Los Gatos in a real nice house and had beautiful cars and three great kids. We both had good jobs. We were both raking in the money. I was working as an account manager, overseeing a million-dollar account. Everything was really good.

"When I was in my early 30s, my husband had an affair with our nanny and things changed. I started to drink. Then one night he hit me and knocked me unconscious onto the kitchen table. I had Chloe, my youngest, in my arms at the time.

"'I'm leaving,' I said. I took Chloe, and he took the boys. Even though I was drinking, I was a very functional alcoholic. I was never the type that passed out on the sofa. I drank when my kids went to bed. I drank at lunch meetings. But no one could ever tell. I was doing good. I still had a job. I had a nice, beautiful penthouse apartment and a new BMW.

"Chloe was very feminine, just like her mom. She had hair down to her waist when she was four. And I used to put it up in a bun every morning. I would put music on in the bathroom, put candles on the bathtub, do her hair up for her—young lady growing up. I was a wonderful mom.

"One night I came home from a trip, and Chloe told me that my husband's brother had raped her in the butt. Chloe was four at the time, and immediately after it happened, he disappeared and was found 40 days later hanging from a tree. If he hadn't

hung himself, I would have killed him! My husband pressured me into not telling anyone. But the day that happened, my life stopped, like my soul broke down.

"I can't really remember clearly, but something like that had happened to me when I was young, too. My aunt told me that my biological father molested me when I was a very little girl. My mother and father separated after that, and my mother married my stepfather. We lived in a nice house. But my mother was a raging alcoholic, so I swore I would never, never drink. 'You're not going to be a woman like your mother,' I always told myself. My stepdad was always angry at me. He wasn't an alcoholic, but he drank to get wasted. To this day, he has a serious temper problem.

"There was always a lot of conflict between my parents: two-by-fours flying through the house, things like that. Breakfast wasn't right, plates going through the kitchen. When I was five, my half-sister was born. We never got along. I had loved being an only child. We lived above a bar. I'd climb downstairs, sit on the barstool, and I'd have Coke® and peanuts for breakfast, get a silver dollar. I was pretty damn happy. I was like the mascot of the bar. People loved to look at me. I was very talented. I was a gymnast, doing flips off the roof from when I was two and a half.

"When I was 15, my mother and stepdad separated, and I moved to Wyoming with my mom. She got into another relationship. One day she said, 'We're moving to Montana. This relationship I'm in is too violent.' I told her, 'I'm not going. I have a boyfriend. And you don't have anyplace for me to live.' She left anyway so I stayed with my boyfriend's grandparents, who kind of became *my family for a while. Life was really good then. I missed school a lot but I wrote my own notes excusing my absences. Basically my mother deserted me, but my life was better without her.*

"After Chloe was raped, I kept thinking about my childhood and how confusing and lonely parts of it had been. I got depressed and was crying a lot. I began to drink more and more. I couldn't fit a wine bottle into my purse, so I started drinking hard liquor, and I could drink all day. I lost my job and my house. I finally went to a residential rehab program because I was tired of hearing about my drinking from my husband, and besides, I didn't have anyplace else to go. I left Chloe with my husband, but I never went back to get her because I was living in my car. How could I take care of her if I didn't have a place? And then I drank even more. I was like counting on the alcohol. I wanted to forget what had happened to Chloe, and everything else. Also, after I left my husband, I had a boyfriend who beat me almost to death.

"I went to jail once, supposedly because I was on drugs when I was taking Chloe out for a visit. It was totally unfair. I pled guilty to child endangerment in order to reduce my sentence. I spent a whole month in jail until I thought I was going to go crazy. Jail was terrible. It was the worst thing I ever saw in my life. I couldn't even eat. I got there and I threw away my food. I thought someone was going to kill me over a piece of bread.

"After I got out, I went into a program, but I couldn't stand it there. I wanted to drink, and besides, I thought, what had my life come to if I needed an alcohol rehab program? So I moved to San Francisco. I lived in cheap hotels. I didn't see my kids at this time because I couldn't take them to a place like that. I was in shock about where my life had gone. I tried to kill myself with

Xanax® and alcohol, but I woke up in the bushes with leaves in my hair. My tolerance was too high. I didn't know where to turn. And I still didn't think I had a problem. I didn't know you couldn't go through deaths, divorce, moving, jail and survive it without any help.

"I had to do something, so I got a job at a jewelry store. I made the best sale of the year. I sold a two-carat diamond. I got to wear all the jewelry I wanted. I got to wear flashy clothes. But I didn't stay there long because I broke my ankle. I was wearing high heels, and I slipped off the curb. I was taken to the hospital and then was referred to the welfare office. While I was there, I met a guy who said, 'Hey, we're having a party at the beach. Why don't you come out?' I said, 'Sure,' even though my leg was casted and I was drinking pretty bad. Then some guy, who had blown up a post office and had spent time in prison, picked me up and took me up to the hills overlooking San Francisco. We lived there for weeks. We would barbecue up there. We came down every few days to take a shower. So we didn't look like we were homeless.

"We would go downtown to eat at St. Anthony's soup kitchen. One day, my wallet got lifted off me. I had it sticking out of my jacket. It had all of our money and food stamps. My boyfriend was so furious, he kicked out a pawnshop window. The whole window came crashing down. We ran and we never got caught. We were like Bonnie and Clyde. We started living in an old army bunker in the cliffs above the beach. You had to climb over the seawall and then scale down about 50 feet, and then jump and roll the other 150 feet to get to it. It was mostly great, but there were mice around that were always disturbing us at night. And I got pneumonia several times from living on the beach.

"Then one day I started feeling really bad. I was getting the shakes, and I was hungry. We went to a very fancy restaurant and ordered the best food and the best bottles of wine on the menu and then disappeared before the check came. We said to each other, 'If we're going to do this, let's do it right.' I had my hair up and blue lipstick on, and the waiter never suspected anything. But soon afterwards, my boyfriend fell off the cliff we were living on and died.

"I had nowhere to go, but his best friend took me in for a while. Unfortunately, he was like some of the men my mother had. He ended up beating my face with a 40-ounce beer bottle and choked me almost to death. I finally got away and was taken to the hospital, and he was arrested and sentenced for five years. After that I went to an alcohol detox program, then worked for the Salvation Army on weekends. So I had enough to live on.

"Then I met a multimillionaire. He was a body builder. He could stop a bus in the middle of the street. People were afraid of him. And I loved it, because he talked to me so sweetly. I never had to worry for a minute. He treated me like a princess. He gave me everything I wanted. If I liked a pair of pants, he'd say, 'Well, buy three pairs.' And if I wanted Godiva® chocolates, okay. He sent me roses that were four feet tall. I'd never been happier in my life. And I was making good money again. But then he started talking about marriage, and his mother opposed it. This big-assed body builder turned out to be a squeak, totally under the thumb of his mother, and he dumped me. While we were going together, I was clean and sober for a couple of years, but then I started taking crack and drinking again.

"I've been to detox so many times, but I never stay more than a day. I hate being there. I feel like I'm being institutionalized.

The staff are so pretentious. They haven't even been to college. They're ex-addicts and they think they know something. They have no clue. They've never even been outside of San Francisco in their lives. Working in a rehab program is the highest they're ever going to go. In one program, a staff member took me to a part of the house that no one knew about and thought it would be a pretty good idea to have sex. Can you believe it? And the program in San Francisco doesn't even feed you right. You can't even get real food there. All they give you is tofu and vegetarian meals, and I hate tofu.

"Four years ago, I got hooked up with the city hospital's case management program. I've been with it since then. My social worker, Lisa, is wonderful. She's the one who got me this beautiful room. I see her every other week and I'm doing much better, but I'm still drinking—minimally, but I don't get drunk. I don't go to bars. I drink in my room. I don't think most people would know I'm drinking.

"Maybe I have to go back to detox to get the alcohol completely out of my system. Maybe I'll drag myself through detox one more time, and bring my food with me this time. I should go, but I can't really do it yet, because I have no one to take care of my cat. I don't have any friends. I used to have a few friends, but they turned out to be drug addicts.

"Chloe is 16 now. She never talks about the rape. Before it, she dressed very feminine. After it, she only wore boys' clothing. That's what she wears now. She dresses very asymmetrical. She won't wear girls' clothing. She's into baseball, football, basketball. She's not feminine whatsoever. She won't talk to me. She and my boys live with their dad.

"A few years ago, I developed lupus, an autoimmune disease. My joints are always painful. I have to take 500 milligrams of morphine a day just to walk. That's how bad the pain is. They drained my knee six times last month. And a few months ago, my computer was stolen. I was starting to write children's books, and all my material was on my computer. So I don't really have much hope for the future. Actually, I don't think about it. I'm too sad. I just think about how I'm going to manage this afternoon. I worry about the TV going out."

I saw Bridgett two months later. She had gone to an alcohol detox program in the interval and was noticeably different— calmer, more logical, more reflective, and able to think more clearly about her future. But when I met with her again nine months after this, she had relapsed. She was stylishly dressed but volatile, she was slurring her words, and she nearly tripped when serving me coffee in her room. She tearfully told me the following, which I have edited for greater coherence:

"A few weeks ago, I went to a party and got a massage from a professional masseur. I suddenly woke up on the massage table and realized the masseur was sodomizing me. I jumped up and screamed that I was being raped. I didn't press charges because no one would have believed me. I started drinking again the next day.

"A week ago, I went to a counselor to talk about the rape. I came home so upset that I felt like cutting my wrists. I told my neighbor, who called the apartment manager, who came to check on me. I didn't want her in my apartment and when she wouldn't leave, I

pushed her out. The apartment management company has just filed papers to have me evicted for assault. So now I am going to lose my apartment. None of this was my fault."

Bridgett also told me that she had lost her cell phone and was now cut off from telephone contact with the outside world. She said she knew she needed to go to alcohol rehab, but it was impossible to make contact with the program without a phone. Besides, there was no one to take care of her cat. And moreover, she said, she couldn't go into a program before her eviction papers were served, which could take up to six months. She could find no way around these obstacles, and whatever solutions I offered, she found reasons that none of them could work.

Six months later, I received a call that Bridgett had died of alcohol poisoning. She had been drinking very heavily for several months, developed pneumonia, left the hospital against medical advice, and was subsequently seen wandering around nude in her apartment building. The social worker from her case management program stayed in touch with her but was helpless to convince her to admit herself to an alcoholic rehab program. The mental health commitment laws made it impossible for Bridgett to be forced into treatment against her will. While an obvious and severe danger to herself, the danger was not considered "imminent," as the law requires for involuntary hospitalization.

One night she accompanied a stranger to his apartment, where they spent the night drinking heavily. He awoke the next morning to find her dead. Her body was already cold.

"I'M IMMUNE TO PAIN IN MY BODY, BUT WHEN SOMEONE HURTS MY FEELINGS, IT MAKES ME FEEL REAL SAD AND I CRY." —ERRADYSE

I came upon Erradyse in Golden Gate Park. She was sitting on the grass. I told her I thought her fur coat looked terrific and was rewarded with a beautiful smile.

"I have to buy myself some new pants, with fishnet, because I've had these pants on for months. And I gotta get my coat cleaned. My coat keeps me warm. I mostly live outside. I can stay indoors for four or five days, and then I have to come out, else I'll die. I die inside. My lungs slow down. I stay in a camper or a van. Sometimes I'm in the hospital and sometimes in jail. And then I have to get out, because if I stay there my veins, my blood cells break and multiply. When I live outside, I start to feel better because I get more oxygen. When it's cold and windy and rainy, I don't get cold. I'm immune to the weather, even in the cold and the rain. I love the outdoors. I survive out here, with the oxygen.

"I don't do drugs or alcohol, so it's not expensive to live. I'm on welfare. Sometimes I beg cigarettes and food. When I'm selling sex, I only ask one time. They say no, I walk away. I don't beg. I charge $40 on up for half and half—suck their dick until it gets hard, and then let them fuck me. In my asshole, it's $60.

"I want the man to stay in me, but they don't. I guess they don't want me to have their baby. I usually tell black men to put a condom on, 'cause I don't want them to think I'm trying to get child support from them, so I mention condom first.

Usually they don't want to use no condom. I don't know how their sperm stays inside of me, but it does. My vagina sucks the sperm out of the man's dick and don't release it. What kinda animal is that? What kinda animal has sex, and the sperm doesn't come out for months and years? It never comes out. It goes into the wall near my ovaries. And then it dies, but it still sits there.

"I've been in San Francisco since 1982. I'm 45 years old. I go to the clinic and get checks up. If I get AIDS, I'll get a blood transfusion. They'll take all my blood out, and they'll put new blood in. Then I'll sweat through my pores. Stay in the hospital for a couple of months. My Medi-Cal will pay for that.

"I got to get this bruise under my eye cleaned. A white girl be disrespecting me. I get in her face. She say, 'Get out of my face.' I say, 'No!' Then we fight, and a man get involved. He punched me. She kicked me all over. It didn't hurt. I don't know why. I'm immune to pain in my body, but when someone hurts my feelings, it makes me feel real sad and I cry. White girls say, 'Get off the street. You can't have no white man. Fuck black men. Don't fuck white men.' They don't want me around. I don't know why they care who's fucking me."

"IF YOU HAVE NO TEETH, IT'S PROOF THAT YOU'VE FUCKED UP REAL BAD—THAT YOU MUST BE NOTHING BUT A FUCK-UP!" —JEFF

"I turn away and cover my mouth when a woman smiles at me. She'd never look at me again if she saw I had no teeth. Even if I got dentures, it wouldn't help, because it's not goin' to fool her. As soon as we kissed, she'd realize it. She'd be completely disgusted and think I'd misled her. She'd drop me like a hot potato. Better not to let anything start. It would be too painful. I've been telling myself, 'Quit looking at women. You're just torturing yourself. It's not gonna happen! You're gonna be alone all your life. It's wicked sad, but that's the way it is.' I'm doomed.

"If you have a big nose, well, no one can blame you. It's just the way you were born. But if you have no teeth, it's proof that you've fucked up real bad—that you must be nothing but a fuck-up!"

Jeff was referred to me by a case management program at San Francisco General Hospital. Shortly before I met him, he had been using drugs heavily and had been living on the street.

"My life didn't start out so good. My mother went nuts when I was five. She heard voices, and was in and out of mental hospitals. Everybody in the neighborhood knew she was crazy. She wouldn't let me have friends over to the house because she was a neat freak and was afraid they'd mess up the house. She always was calling me a 'no good son of a bitch.' Sometimes she'd take after my father with a knife. I was always afraid she'd kill me.

"My sister ran away from home when I was six. My parents sent me out to find her, but it was hopeless. We never heard from her again. My parents were totally indifferent.

"My father was my hero. He was a garbage collector—the best in the city. He never even left a gum wrapper on the ground. I became a garbage collector, too. I worked and paid taxes for 12 years. But one day I was caught with a tiny bit of pot in my urine and was fired on the spot. It was ridiculous!

"Being a garbage man was everything to me. When I lost that, I lost everything! I got so depressed I could barely get out of bed. One day I started using crack, and then heroin. In no time I burned through all my money, lost my apartment, and lost my connection to my family. I also lost my fiancée, but I suppose I didn't deserve her anyway. I was nothing but a worthless piece of shit.

"For the next 10 years, I slept over a heating vent on the sidewalk. When it rained, I'd hop onto someone's porch to stay dry. Living on the street is so bad, you have to be either stoned or crazy to bear it. And San Francisco is a fuckin' cold, foggy city.

"During those years, I nearly died a couple of times from overdoses. I couldn't get through a day without a fix; I'd get real sick. When you're on heroin, you just can't let that happen. You'll do anything to prevent it. You can't think of anything except drugs and trying to stay alive. I tried panhandling in the early days, but that takes too much patience and is completely unreliable. Even in the best of days, it doesn't pay enough for your heroin. Most days, if you got $10 panhandling, you were lucky. I supported my habit by shop-lifting. I'd go into stores,

couldn't look her in the face anymore after all she had done for me. It's totally corny, but it was the only way I could show her what she meant to me. If it weren't for Lisa, I'd be dead.

"I've been clean for six months now, the first time in 10 years. I've started volunteering at an animal shelter 'cause I'm getting sick of doing nothing except watching TV. I also adopted this neat little kitten. She's my best friend. I've also started to think about what else I want to do with my life. Maybe I'll live 'til 50."

I saw Jeff six months after this last conversation. He was still free of drugs and had begun working as a paid, part-time administrative staff member in the program that had saved his life.

"I DON'T SLEEP. I DON'T EAT." —MICHAEL

At first I thought I was looking at a bundle of rags. But then it moved, and I saw a pair of eyes peeking out from behind a hood. As I turned to him, he began talking softly to himself and then more loudly to the bell that clanged in the tower of the Ferry Building at 15-minute intervals.

"Who are you talking to?" I asked him.
"God," he responded.
"How do you get in touch with him?" I pursued.
"Through the bell," he whispered, and abruptly stood up and walked away, pushing his cart in front of him.

I saw him again a few days later, when he was more loquacious.

"I'm a Jehovah's Witness. I wrote an art book. You can look it up in the Library of Congress."

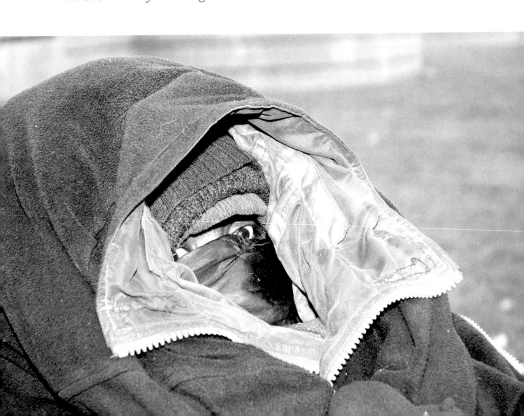

"I went to barber school and learned to grow women's hair. I don't cut it, I grow it."

"I was born in DC, and I never left. And I'm never going to leave. I walked from DC to San Francisco. It took me a few weeks."

"Last night I slept with my wife. She sleeps in Israel. I don't want to say her name. She's a Jehovah's Witness."

"I don't sleep. I don't eat. I breathe. You know President Obama? He never sleeps. Jesus never sleeps. He just takes a sword. God helps me."

"Would you like an orange?"
He wouldn't take no for an answer and handed me not one, but two.

"MY MOTHER MUST HAVE KNOWN WHAT MY FATHER WAS DOING EVEN BEFORE HE RAPED ME."

—REBECCA

"I first got depressed in my 20s. Everything seemed crowded up and dark in my head. I didn't have delusions, but I just felt terrible and like I was always running on empty.

"I got married during those years, but it didn't work out. I was out of whack emotionally. I let him talk me into it because I thought I loved him, but it didn't last.

"I became real depressed again a few times in my 30s and had to be hospitalized. Then I got a heart attack, but I survived it and was still doing okay and still working. But when I was 38, I was in a real bad wreck. One of those big, long trucks hit the back of my car. I flipped underneath the steering wheel and slammed my head. Ever since then I don't think as clearly and can't remember things as well. I have trouble adding and subtracting. I can't figure out the change I owe when I'm in a store, and I get very confused when I'm under even a little stress. I used to be very smart. I had gotten a full scholarship to college when I was 18 and worked as a typist for 22 years.

"The truck accident was a real disaster for me. Not only was my ability to think hurt, but I was never able to forget the moment that the truck hit me. For 10 years, I had nightmares about it when I was asleep and flashbacks when I was awake. Whenever I saw or heard a large truck, I went into a panic. I'm getting better now because I'm taking Prozac, but I still get scared and my heart races when I see a truck.

"When I was in my 40s, I started having problems with an old injury to my leg that had occurred when I had fallen off my bike at 16. I began to have trouble walking. I had to retire early from my job.

"I didn't expect to be homeless, but my Social Security didn't carry me. I found myself in a mess that I couldn't get out of. I had enough money for rent, but I didn't have enough to pay for the security deposit, so I could never get a room. I tried to save my money by living in a shelter three weeks of the month. I spent the last week on a bus going back and forth to Reno. You could get a very cheap ticket then. I kind of used the bus as a moving shelter.

"I guess I also left during that last week of the month because I needed to run around. I'd get real excited, thinking I was going to save my money for a room, and I'd do a lot of running. I mean, I was actually running, even with my bad leg. I was free, no roof over my head, and no restrictions and rules to follow. It was difficult to sleep during that week, maybe because I was drinking a lot of coffee. It was a wonderful, exhilarating feeling, but I also felt kind of crazy. The doctors told me I had manic depression. That's how I lived for eight years, in and out of shelters and buses.

"Three years ago, I broke my ankle while I was walking off a curb. And a year later I developed cancer of the ovaries. It spread to my lungs and my liver, but I think the radiation treatment they gave me stopped it from spreading further. Then a few months ago, I broke my wrist getting off a bus. That's what this cast on my right arm is all about. So I've had a difficult few years.

"But the good part is that I got into a special psychiatry program at San Francisco General Hospital. The social worker I got, Lisa, has been wonderful. She gave me this stuffed animal when I was going for my radiation. And she's the one who got me this room. The rent is supported by the city. Things have been much more stable since I moved in here. My nightmares are better, probably because I'm now on Prozac.

"I'm not depressed anymore, and my anxiety is much better. I've come a long way from where I started.

"I didn't come from the best family. My father died when I was two. I can't remember him exactly, but I was told by my grandmother that he used to carry me around a lot and used to take me to work and everything. He kind of protected me from my mother. After he died, I was at her mercy. She didn't watch us that closely. I got hurt a lot as a kid. When I was three, I crawled over to the floor heater and fell on it. I got third-degree burns. I don't know where my mother was at the time. Maybe she was in the hospital. She went insane about then and had to be committed for a year. She was real depressed. She cried and yelled a lot. I'd be real embarrassed about it. My grandparents took care of us then.

"We tried getting back together as a family later on, but it didn't work out. My mother was still not right in her head, and she married a man who was really abusive. I was six years old. I remember that year because it was the year I broke my arm. My stepfather drank a lot and was real violent. He had guns and things. He was sexually abusive, too. He was real forward and everything to me and my sister. Mostly he just touched me and messed around, but it went on for several years.

"When I was 12, he got real bad. He jumped on me in the middle of the night and tore me open, and I had to be sewn up. We went to court over that. And the judge told me the next time it happened, to get one of those guns and shoot him. But he only got a year in jail. The judge seemed to be on his side even though he could see I couldn't help myself because I had been asleep when my stepfather came into my room. I blame my mother because she must have known what my father was doing even before he raped me. But I guess it was hard for her because she was so depressed.

"After that, my mother separated from him, but he still had visitation rights when he got out of jail. The strange thing is that I had forgotten about the rape until his death last year. It was always present as a kind of dark memory, but I couldn't recall the details until my sister told me he had died. He got away with a lot in his life.

"I guess the only real parent I had was my father, for my first two years. I don't have a real picture of him in my mind, but I have a sense of him, a kind of warm feeling of someone being there. I use the sensation to comfort myself sometimes. When things get out of hand, when I've had a big day or when I'm in a lot of pain or when the stress builds up, I try to remember that someone was once close by. It's helped me survive."

"I'M GOIN' TO SELL THESE SHOES FOR $10,000."

—THE SHOE SALESMAN

"Let me give you a shoeshine," he said as I passed him on Market Street.
"You got it,' I responded. *"How much do you charge?"*
"One dollar for a shine."
"I can do better than that for you."
"No, I'm just trying to make an honest living. I make $60 a month."

He held up a pair of women's shoes and asked me if I wanted to buy them.
"See these shoes? These are the world's greatest shoes. I'm goin' to sell these shoes for $10,000, and that will get me off the street. I've shined and sold shoes most of my life. I call myself a 'buffeton.'"
"What is that?" I asked.
"Someone who buffs shoes. I'm here three days a week. The other days, I have a second job. I take care of police horses. I'm also a certified public accountant. I live in a church. They let me sleep in an office. My sister pays my rent. Do you like my beard?"
"I like it."
"So do I. It keeps the dogs away."

"I sell shoes to the yoga pimps. Yoga pimps don't pimp women. They pimp yachts."
"What do you mean?"
"Well, it's better than saying 'bubera.' And I don't know what 'bubera' means, but it's not as bad as saying 'yoga pimp.'"

"When black men come, the police come and take their shoes. They sell their shoes, and they think that's the way to make money. That's the law of a physician that makes it seem like he's married. That's the way I make money."

He went on in this vein, polishing and shining my shoes, always talking in an animated manner, stopping his story only to ask me occasionally if I wanted to have a drink of his herb mixture. This, he said, was very healthy but "too tight for him." He told me that he had been hospitalized in psychiatric units many times but is doing fine now. His sister is helping him.

My 10-year-old tennis sneakers had never looked better than after his 20-minute shine, for which, and despite my protests, he would take only one dollar. I stayed to chat for an hour, not that I understood much of his conversation. I was enchanted by his warmth and friendliness.

This man seemed to be making out okay at the moment and survived partially because of his spirit, his warmth, his infectious enthusiasm, his great sense of humor, and his enjoyment of hard work. In fact, he seemed to love and take pride in his work far more than most other people on the planet. He was certainly more friendly and outgoing than most. For whatever reasons, his mental illness hadn't sucked him dry. His life was evidence that even in its fairly severe form, mental illness doesn't have to completely sink people, especially if they have family to rely on.

"TOO MANY PEOPLE ARE DEAD HERE."

—Woman from Honolulu

I came upon this woman struggling with her possessions down Market Street. She politely but firmly refused my offer of help.

"I came from Honolulu a long time ago. I'm going to move out of San Francisco. Too many people are dead here. Six thousand people suddenly dead. People suddenly dead in Santa Rosa, too. I sleep outside most nights because I don't feel safe inside."

"AFTER MY FIRST KILL, IT GOT TO BE NOTHING."

—WALTER

"There's a cop who works for the San Rafael police department whose job it is to hunt the homeless. He rides around the back roads in the hills and finds those of us who live in camps in the woods. If he finds us, he writes us a ticket and moves us out."

I met Walter at the end of the Blithedale Avenue exit ramp from the highway. I had seen him many times at the same spot, which by some unwritten agreement with his colleagues he seemed to own. He explained to me that when anyone else was there panhandling, it was by his consent.

He wasn't interested in talking with me at first, partially because it was hard for him to talk and work at the same time. Specifically, I was distracting him from making eye contact with the drivers and was interfering with his business. He worked there six hours a day, rain or shine, sometimes making only $15—on a good day $50, but on average $20. When I asked him what it was like to stand in the rain and make only $15, which I calculated was $2.50 an hour and represented the total proceeds from 25,000 cars coming off the ramp during that particular day (or .06 cent per car), he answered philosophically that some days were bound to be good and others bad. *"If I have a bad day, I know there will be a good day sometime soon."*

He ultimately warmed up to me and after 15 minutes led me to a little grove of trees under the highway that he used as a place where he could rest, smoke, and get away from the relentless traffic.

"I had a place in the woods on the hill. Hell, I had it for 10 years. The police finally found me by helicopter one night using an infrared sensor. They seem to have nothing better to do than hunt the homeless camps. If they come on us, we have one hour to move and then they come back with a whole crew and take all your shit. They're not allowed to take your water, but they take everything else. And if you've set up good and you've been there for a while, there's no way you can move all of your stuff in one hour. I've lost everything I owned in six camps to them: sleeping bags, tents, food, everything. That's a lot of stuff to lose. You have to stay hidden real good. We can't have a fire and we can't use lights except for flashlights, and then we have to keep these real low. It seems like I'm always in hiding. It's like Nam.

"I was in Nam for four years. I was 18 when I was drafted. I was on a patrol boat as the rear gunner. We were a floating target every day we went out. And every day we wondered whether it would be our last. We used a lot of pot and booze to quiet our nerves. After a while I stopped feeling as scared because it got to be routine. The good thing is that we would never be attacked without some warning. You always knew when you were going to be shot at because you could smell the sweet opium that the Cong used. Also, you would see sniper fire from the trees. And then you just turn the machine guns on them and cut them down.

"My first kill, it was hand-to-hand fighting. I had a knife with a long blade, a kind of bayonet. He had one, too. He made a big mistake, and I slit his throat. And then I threw up. After my first kill, it got to be nothing. You become an expert because you train and train and train.

"The only other time I threw up was after I killed a kid. It made me sick. He was only seven years old, but he was armed to the teeth. He had a grenade hidden under his arm. He raised his elbow and let the grenade drop and then ran for the trees. I only had a few seconds to get rid of the grenade, and then I blew a hole in his chest seven inches wide with my rifle.

"Even though you get used to having your life in danger every day, it was still no joke. You depended on your buddies, but you didn't want to get too close to them. You joked around at night and drank beers and smoked pot and stuff but never got to know them too well. You didn't want to make friends because friends die.

"When I was in the jungle, I was always loaded. I had two ankle guns, two side pistols, an M-16, an M-14, and knives. When I came back from Nam, it was really rough. I had nightmares every single night. Every time a car backfired I hit the ground, thinking it was an incoming explosive. I was ready to kill, but I didn't have anything to do it with. I felt totally naked. The PTSD program at the VA hospital really helped me. Going through my story over and over again finally took away the nightmares, but it took years.

"I started drinking before I went to Nam. Every weekend was a party in my parents' house. Both of them drank, and my sister was an alcoholic. After I went to Nam, I began to drink more heavily, and when I returned to the States, I drank even more to quiet my nerves, help me sleep, and take away the nightmares. I was a heavy drinker for 30 years. Two years ago, I found out *that I had hepatitis C. It hit me that my life was really on the line. I stopped drinking cold turkey.*

"You won't see me here much anymore because I saved up enough to rent a trailer. It will be the first time I've been inside since I came back from Nam."

"I SLEEP WHERE THE FROG PEOPLE LIVE." —RHONDA

Rhonda was sitting on a box outside a restaurant, talking to herself and trying to keep warm with her jacket and the extra pair of pants someone had given her. She had been sleeping on the street for months, although she had been given a room when she was last discharged from the psychiatric unit. *"I just didn't want to stay in that room."* Her parents and seven brothers and sisters live a few miles away. They bring her food three times a month but don't want to take her in. *"I don't know why they don't want me."*

When I initially approached her, she was shy, diffident, hesitant, and almost inaudible, but when I asked about her family, her whole personality changed.

"My family came from Puerto Rico, Norway, Jerusalem, somewhere else. We were once rich, but some people followed us home and then played all kinds of goddamn sorts of tricks on us and took everything we had. They gave us a lot of bullshit, a lot of junk and goddamn trash, and stole every goddamn thing we looked at.

"My family didn't come from goddamn anywhere and didn't have goddamn nothing when we arrived. We had no goddamn body else. We had no goddamn mother or father.

"I sleep where the frog people live—on the beaches. They combine with real frogs. Seafood, that's what I mean, heliomonsters and all of that, hamburger monsters. They kill you for hamburgers."

THE GANG: MAX, SABRINA, AND JED

I came upon Max, Sabrina, and Jed one raw fall morning in Golden Gate Park. They were huddled together, shivering, trying to warm themselves by passing around a bottle of some greenish alcoholic mix. As a group, they were a bit intimidating to approach, but summoning my courage, I commented to them on how cold it was, and they affably reached back to me. By the end of a day of hanging out with them, I had more or less been included in their little gang. However, as the afternoon sun dropped behind the trees, and San Francisco's cold fog began blowing in, I became increasingly self-conscious about the warm home and real dinner I would return to that evening. They would spend that night and the next night, and the next, shivering in doorways. Unaccountably, they didn't seem to begrudge me my life of privilege, revealing much more generosity than I would have been able to muster had I been in their shoes.

"I'M NOT PROUD OF SOME OF THE SHIT I DID." —MAX

Max was a loud, foul-mouthed, funny alpha male who dominated the whole scene, deciding where they sat, what they drank, when they came, and when they went. No one else spoke when he was carrying forth. Everything was for show: his stories, his tattoos, his antics. What was true and what wasn't? Who could tell?

"I spent 14 years in the marines. I was a corpsman in Vietnam. My great-granddaddy was in the Civil War, and my daddy was head of cardiology in the navy. I lost both of my sons in Iraq. So I feel totally fucked.

"You wanna hear something? This broke my goddamn heart. When I was in Nam, a guy named Joe Eliot came back from patrol. He had 13 days left on his tour of duty. I don't know what the fuck happened. He sat right next to me. He pulled out his gun, put it to his head, and blew his brains out. They say that the last couple of weeks of duty, people are vulnerable. The last few days, that's either when you get blown up or take your own life.

"Well, I'll tell you something. I killed people in Nam. Someone fucked me over when I was in prison. I had gasoline smuggled in and set him on fire. I'm not proud of that! I fuckin' despise violence now.

"I had this crazy Native American Indian buddy who wrapped a cloth around an arrow, stuck it in some Crisco®, lit it, and shot it a mile. I swear to God! He stood out on the patio, pulled that bow back 65 pounds. 'Don't do it. Don't fuckin' do it, man!' I said. He knew exactly what he was going to do. He said, 'Watch this!' Famous last words, right? 'Trust me on this one,' he said. That goddamn fucker went 1,000 meters as the crow flies! It looked like a comet, man. Within two minutes, we heard sirens. That motherfucker! The arrow had landed on someone's roof and set the house on fire. 'You crazy-assed Indian!' I said."

"NOW I'M HERE, AND I'M NOT QUITE SURE WHERE I'M GOING." —SABRINA

Sabrina was a sweet, gentle, quiet woman who sat shaking, with a blanket wrapped around her. Occasionally, she'd break out laughing at Max's jokes. At other times, she'd become tearful.

"I'm new at this homeless thing. I just got here on Saturday— from Lincoln, California. Twenty-six dollars was what I had, and it just about paid for a one-way ticket here, so I got on the bus and came. Now I'm here, and I'm not quite sure where I'm going.

"I was living with my boyfriend in Lincoln. He was my best friend for 15 years before we started living together. But then things went bad. He was taking speed and slamming me around a bit. We broke up. Then we got back together. We went back and forth, back and forth. Two months ago, I spent a week cleaning him up, and right away he starting tweaking. I hadn't been drinking for 31 days, but as soon as I found out he was using, I began drinking again.

"I started going downhill fast, so I went to a Christian alcohol rehab facility. As soon as I got out, I called my boyfriend and found that he was living with my closest girlfriend. So I lost my lover and my girlfriend, the two closest people to me. I felt completely betrayed. A friend took me in, but I started stealing from her liquor cabinet. I got a little money and came to San Francisco. And I guess I'm here trying to numb myself.

"I come from a long line of alcoholics. I've drunk all my life, even though I had two jobs and went to college at the same time. I was three weeks away from getting my bachelor's. I did all that while I was raising three kids. It's all gone now.

"I'm not close to my parents. I don't know who my real dad is, but my stepdad molested me for two years, starting when I was 13. My stepdad and mom are still together even though I eventually told my mother what he did. I didn't tell her at the time because I felt too guilty. I blamed myself. It doesn't matter how right or wrong it is, when someone's touching you like that, you have certain reactions. It felt good. He came in the night, and I pretended I was asleep.

"I hated my mom. She was a prude about sex and once told me she didn't even like it. I blamed her for my dad coming in, 'cause I thought if she had sex with my stepdad, he would have left me alone. I also hated her because she should've known. How do you not know something like that? It was her responsibility to know, and you know, protect your kids.

"Some people say that when a father or stepfather does that kind of thing, it makes it impossible for a girl to like sex, but it didn't seem to have that effect on me. I became promiscuous as a teen-ager and liked it. As soon as I graduated from high school, I left, and I got pregnant.

"I've been up all night and I'm freezing. It might also be a bit of the DTs."

"I CAME TO SAN FRANCISCO TO DIE." —JED

Jed didn't say a word for the first two hours I spent with him and the gang, but once drawn out, he was exceedingly reflective.

"Once you've been in prison, it's like a life sentence because it follows you for the rest of your days. I haven't been convicted of a crime in nine years, but I still can't get a job. I'm tired and down, and there's not much I can do about it. Prozac helped level me out for a while, but then it stopped working. I do stupid shit out here. I know better. I just get drunk and don't care.

"Some guys have the mountains in their blood. They come down to a city, but they always go back to the mountains. For me, it's the streets. Out here, nothing matters. I came to San Francisco to die. My only hope is that I'll die drunk and never feel any pain."

"SOMEONE BROKE INTO MY HOTEL ROOM AND STOLE MY EYE." —ROSE

"My mother never liked me. When I was 12, the guy she was living with began molesting me. I didn't tell her because I knew she wouldn't do a damn thing. The whole neighborhood knew what was going on.

"A year later, I got pregnant and had a son by some other guy. I didn't know how to protect myself because my mother never taught me. When I was 14 I began jumping out of my bedroom window and seeing George, who was 30 years older than me. When my mom found out, she threw all my clothes on the street, gave me $5, and told me to leave. I moved in with George and ended up becoming the mother of three boys and three girls.

"I left George because he used to beat me up so bad. Once he stabbed me in the neck. After I moved out, he snuck into my house one night and tried to kill me on account of him being jealous. He shot at me four times with a revolver. One bullet hit my forehead. I had our baby in my arms and our little girl next to me. If I hadn't leaned back, he would have killed his own baby.

"When I got older, I got into the drug life in a big way. See these needle marks? Then I began doing crack and turning tricks to pay for it. It's lucky I don't have AIDS. If I met a guy and his wife was sick or something and he just wanted to do his little thing, and go about his business, and if he treated me all right, then fine. I'd do it with him, and that's it. But if he tried to misuse me, I'd set his ass on fire.

"I was homeless off and on for years. I'd sleep in doorways and sometimes in cardboard boxes. I know what it's like to be cold. It's why I give homeless people my blankets and my clothes.

"I used to read a lot. But a few years ago, my right eye got infected and the doctor had to take it out. I've been wearing a prosthesis since then. Once I had it sitting in a glass of water beside my bed. Someone broke into my hotel room and stole it. Can you believe it? Stole my own eye from my own room!

"Women who had love as children are happy. Sometimes I watch them in front of the hotel, laughing and joking and

having a good time. I can't join in because I don't fit. I never had nobody to cry to, nobody to talk to. I never had a girlfriend. I don't know what it is about me, what it is I do wrong. Must be something. I'm lonely all the time. Sometimes I try to buy friendship with crack, sometimes with sex. I keep putting myself out there and getting hurt. Even someone bad is better than being alone.

"I'm scared to do drugs by myself because I'm afraid I might try to kill myself. I know that I'd be taking the easy way out, but I lay up two or three days in my room, and just want out. I want to go through that door, but I'm scared to do it. Every time I'm at the subway station, and the train is comin' down the track, I feel like that train is calling me to jump. And I have to physically grab hold of something to stop myself. Drugs become your comfort, your friend, a bad friend. They're supposed to make you forget, but I don't forget. I still be empty inside. I just go 'round the corner and cry to myself. I know time is not long for me.

"I so much want a puppy that I could I talk to, that I can love. I'd feed him before I fed myself. It would fill up my heart. I'm afraid to volunteer at a pet place because I'd be afraid either that I'd kidnap some dog or that I'd fall in love with it and then I'd lose it."

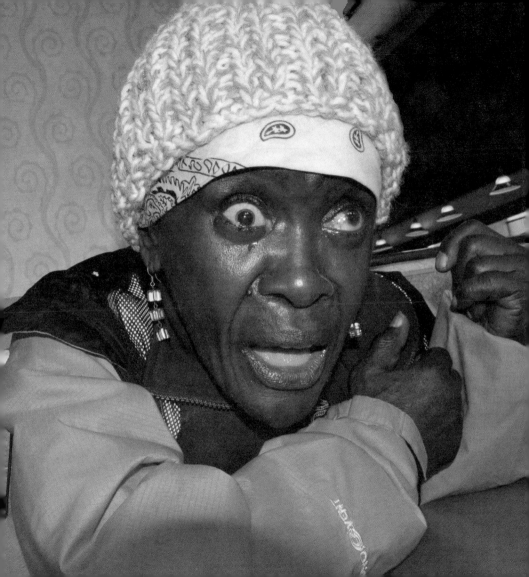

"IT'S HARD HAVING A RELATIONSHIP WHEN YOU'RE LIVING ON THE STREET." —DONNA

"I've been homeless for 13 years, since I lost my job as a maid in a hotel. I've lived in the same spot outside for 10 years. I'm eligible for GA [General Assistance], but I can't get it because I have a bail warrant out for my arrest and if I went into the welfare office, I'd get picked up and put in jail. My original offense was possession of crack, and I got out on bail. I didn't go back to court because I was afraid I'd be convicted and have to go to jail. I haven't been in jail that much, about five times in my whole life, but I hate it.

"If I had the money, I'd live in an SRO [single-room-occupancy hotel]—if it didn't have roaches or rats. But those places are often terrible. When my boyfriend and I first got to San Francisco and started living in a room, I'd have to stay up all night long, sitting on the window sill with a fishing pole and poke the rats out of the bed so my boyfriend could get a good night's sleep and get up for work the next morning. It's not that there were so many rats, but one, in my opinion, is too many. They don't bother me as long as I see them coming, you know. When they run up on you, that's when it's bad.

"I wash my hands a thousand times a day, but they still get dirty digging in the garbage. It's easy to get sick when you live on the streets. I just got out of the hospital yesterday for pneumonia and a hernia.

"But I find all kinds of things in the garbage. I found these shoes that I'm wearing. Once, years ago, I was looking in a garbage can for a tissue to blow my nose, and I found this leather purse

with a $10, $20, and a $100 bill in it. Another time I found a wallet with a credit card. It was a corporate credit card, unlimited. We got sleeping bags, iPods, everything. Being the honest citizen that I am, I put the wallet in the mailbox.

"If I had kept all the blankets, sleeping bags, and backpacks I've found over the years, I could open my own sports shop. But it's all been stolen. Homeless people steal from homeless people. If you turn your back for one second, your things are gone. Blankets are especially tough, because they're too heavy to lug around all day and you're forced to stash them someplace. When you come back to get them at night, sometimes they're there and sometimes they're not. Today I was sleeping over on that bench, and someone stole my cigarettes, my food, and my lighter. And they were right beside me!

"It's hard having a relationship when you're living on the street. My boyfriend always wants his way. I tell him he's got an attitude. But he's adorable—strawberry blond and built like a brick shithouse. He's 44, 10 years younger than me. We both smoke crack, which makes us irritable, and we have different hustles, you know. He likes to go on binges and be up for three or four days, but I can't really do that. When he's been awake for too long, he gets mad at everything. Crack is the only thing I do, but he mixes it with other drugs. Another problem is that he's been in jail over and over again for theft, and he's also violated his parole in Delaware, so he's always worried that he'll be picked up.

"Also, he's not a morning person. This morning, he got grouchy because the department of public works sprayed the sidewalk and wet my half of the blanket. I wanted to share his half, which made him irritable. The last person I had a relationship with wasn't a morning person either. He broke four of my ribs with his fist over a disagreement we had about a taco one morning. We're still best friends. I should have known better than to argue with him in the morning.

"Living on the streets is not so bad. I'm a survivor. My mother left me right after I was born, and I guess I'm doing all right. I love to read. That's mostly what I do. In five years, I'll probably be doing the same thing: just reading and tryin' to make it."

"THE DEVIL IS HERE!" —MARIA

I was walking down Mission Street and came upon a woman struggling to get into her house with a key. I asked if I could help, at which moment her mother opened the door, discovered that I was a psychiatrist, and with an insistency that could not easily be resisted, invited me into their house.

The daughter had been hospitalized in the psychiatric ward at the city hospital several times, and was taking medication that had been prescribed for her at a public outpatient clinic.

The father had died the previous year, and mother and daughter were struggling to make ends meet, keep up the house, and pay their medical bills. The daughter repeatedly expressed her fear that the hospital would refuse to treat her if she couldn't pay her bills.

Speaking mostly in Spanish, and constantly talking over each other, the two women took me by the hand from room to room, and with warm hospitality and enormous pride, showed me each one of their hundreds of religious objects and paintings. At various points, the daughter talked about the Devil.

"The Devil is here! I don't want to know anything about the Devil. I hear voices, but I don't bother with them. I have the head and beard of Christ right in my room. The Devil came into the house because my sister brought in bad underwear. God took away everything. Something happened, but I don't know what. Jesus keeps the Devil small."

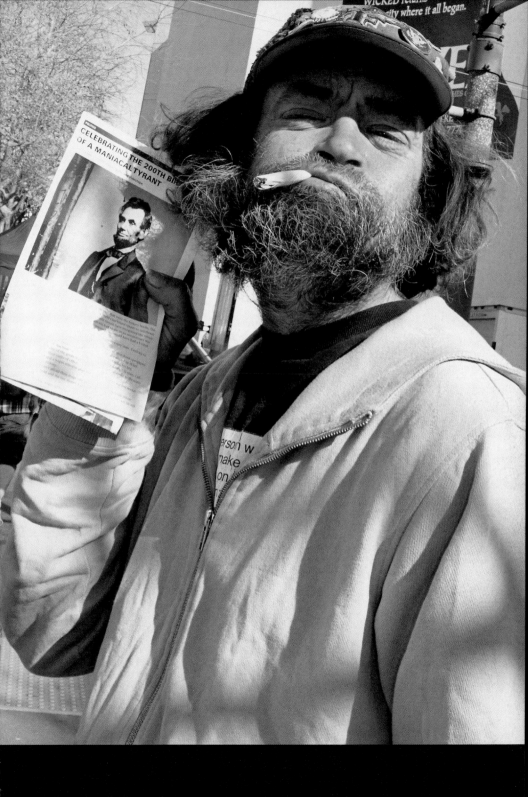

CELEBRATING THE 200TH BIRTHDAY
OF A MANIACAL TYRANT

"WHENEVER I LIVE INSIDE, I START THINKING ABOUT WHAT I'VE LOST." —JONATHAN

I met this man on Howard Street lugging a cart behind him. He had alcohol on his breath, and he had a blank look on his face until he began talking about what had happened in his life.

"I was married for 15 years. I had two children. I worked as a mechanic. Things were good. About 20 years ago, I found my wife sleeping with my best friend. I got depressed, started drinking, and couldn't stop. I lost my job and began living on the streets. I've never been able to go back.

"Whenever I live inside, I start thinking about what I've lost. When I live outside, I have to keep thinking about where I'm going to get my next meal, where I'm going to sleep, who's trying to steal from me. I don't have time to think about the mess I've made of my life."

MAN WITH A CANE — JESSIE

I met Jessie in his tiny, musty hotel room, where he had lived for many years. He had a serious organic brain disorder, probably a result of his heavy drinking and head injuries from alcohol-related falls. Despite the fact that the alcohol was slowly killing him, and he was hanging onto life by a slender thread, he continued to drink, and at the time I met him, he had tripped in the street and broken his arm and leg. He managed to survive for some time with the help of his social worker, a meals-on-wheels program, and other supportive services.

Eventually, one December, he was admitted to the public hospital in San Francisco. Through the tenacious efforts of the hospital social worker, his son and daughter were located in Texas. He was moved to a nursing home near them. Without alcohol and in a more structured living situation, he is reportedly doing better than at any time in the past 10 years.

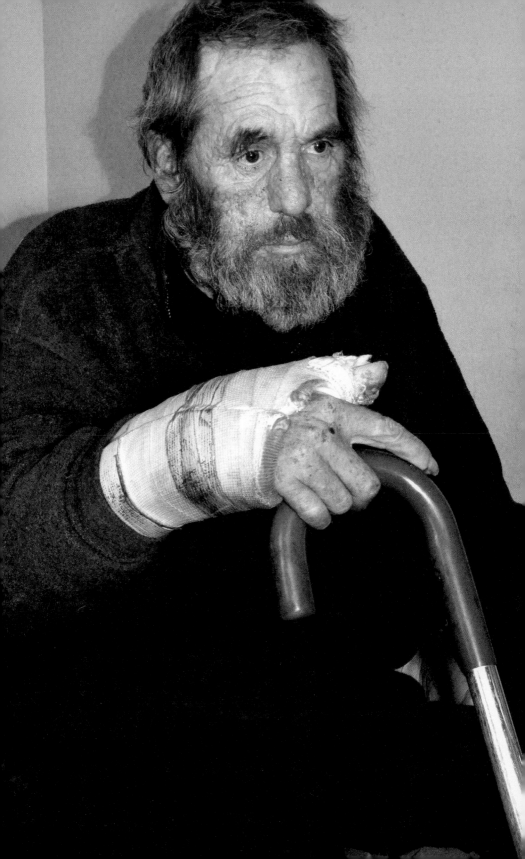

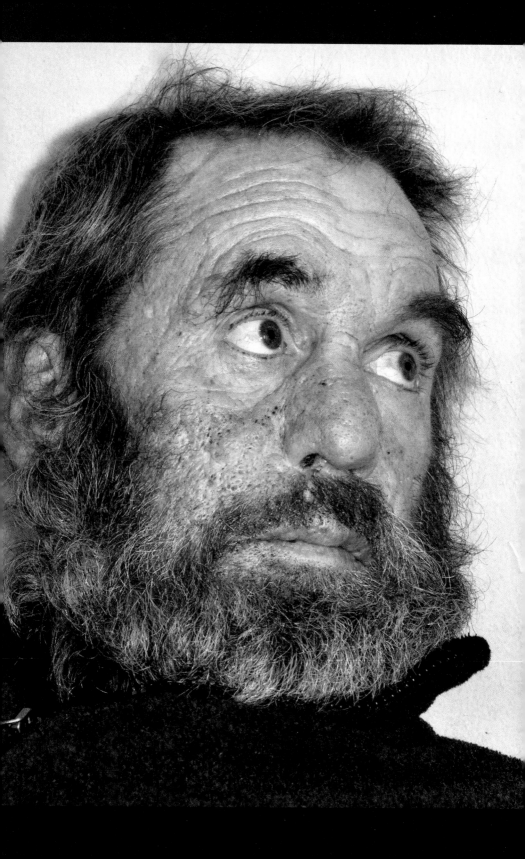

"MY MAMA TRADED MY BICYCLE FOR A SIX-PACK OF BOOZE." —LEE

"I came from Louisiana. My mama and daddy had a lot of mouth when they were drunk. One night when I was only a kid, she found him at a bar, pulled him outside, and tried to run him down with her car. Another night he came home drunk and my three sisters and me, we were so scared that we hid in the bathroom until he went to sleep.

"One Christmas when I was seven, we all got bicycles from the welfare department. A few days later, we come home from school and couldn't find 'em. 'Mama, where are our bikes?' 'Oh, I don't know,' she said. I learned later that she had traded my bicycle for a six-pack of booze.

"One afternoon, she and her sister got drunk and started fightin'. My mama hauled off and broke her sister's jaw. She needed pins to keep her jaw together for three months.

"The neighbors would see us walkin' down the road and would yell at us, 'Well, your mama is nothin' but a bootleggin' whore. She got every man in the house drinkin' and doing it with her.' I couldn't defend myself or her or what went on in the house 'cause I had such a bad stutterin' problem that nobody 'cept one of my sisters could understand me. I felt helpless, like I was in an empty, dark room, in a dark spot, dark ring line. My mama didn't have patience with my stuttering. And my daddy would just laugh at me. I carried that with me all my life.

"We used to go 'round the neighborhood beggin' for food 'cause we was always hungry. It was hard to concentrate on books when all we could think about was our stomachs. Sometimes

we got lucky and the teachers gave us food. When we'd asked my mama for food, she'd tell us to look in the 'frigerator. When we told her there was none, she'd say, 'Go over to your auntie's house and ask her.' But our auntie didn't have any more food than we did, because she was always drunk, same as my mama.

"When I was 11, the school called the welfare department about us. A woman came out to our house, but she didn't come back for a year. Finally, we were put in foster care. My foster mom wanted to adopt me because of the money she'd get paid. My foster daddy wanted to adopt me because they had no boys, and he wanted a son. So he's looking out on that. So I got lucky. I got a family.

"Once when I went back to visit my mama, I found her locked in the bathroom, tryin' to drink herself to death. They took her to the hospital. The doctors wanted to give her medicine. I told 'em, 'She has a drinkin' problem and a drawback problem—drawing back from her family. You can dope her up with medicine all you like and it ain't goin' to change nothin'. Because she has a gene for the disease, and your medicine ain't going to do nothin' for that gene.' Drawback is like a door shuttin' in your face. Like a wall that puts you in a hole and shuts the door on you, shuts it on you. You see, when you have a drawback, you don't want to do anything. You don't want to cook, you don't want to associate, all you want to do is sit in your room and cry. My sister had the gene, too, because she has a drawback problem. Her husband would go into her room and say to her, 'Judy, we is all hungry.' She don't look up, she don't answer, so he'd go to the Chinese restaurant and bring back some food. When he married her, he didn't know she had it, didn't know nothin' about her. 'Well, now you know!' I tell him.

"I've lived in different places, and now I'm here, livin' on the streets, luggin' this cart around with me. The rubber is comin' off its wheels, but I put duct tape around it. I spend a lot of time at Bible studies at church and that's where I get a lot of my food. But flashbacks of things I blocked as a child come back on me. I can't seem to get away from 'em. You don't miss nothin' as a child."

"LIFE ON THE STREETS ISN'T EASY, BUT IT'S NOT DESPERATELY HARD."

I came across this woman talking to herself and doing a crossword puzzle.

"Life on the streets isn't easy, but it's not desperately hard. I'm sleeping on the streets and eating out of garbage cans. I have two or three spots that I sleep, but I don't want to say where. I tried to get on SSI, but I couldn't get on the list, or whatever. That's all I want to talk about."

talk except to tell me ~~she had been kept in a psych~~ ward and had been given meds that made her itch so badly that she couldn't stop scratching her face.

"EVERYONE SAYS HOW TOUGH IT IS TO BE HOME-LESS, BUT I'M GOOD AT IT." —VINCE

"I lived at the Mission Hotel for five years. What you get for almost your whole welfare check is a tiny room with a public bathroom. I liked the other residents, but I couldn't take the lice, the roaches, the bedbugs, the mice. I always had the feeling I was being eaten alive. One night a bedbug had a feast on my blood. He could hardly walk he was so full and fat. He had made a total pig of himself. The hotel disinfected the room, but after that, I was so afraid of being infected again by someone who might be bringing bedbugs into my room, I wouldn't let anyone sit on my bed.

"My woman, Linda, wouldn't stay there with me after the bedbugs bit her. She wasn't goin' for that. Also, it seemed like every time she came over, the mice wanted to come out and play. Also, the roaches would always be munching on things when she was there. She'd wake up and say, 'Take me home!'

"The Mission is the largest welfare hotel in the city. It has more than 300 people. About 50 percent of the people are mentally ill. If you add the drug addicts, it's much more. Most of the people, they're very low-functioning. Some have been there for years. Basically, they can't afford anything else or they have no place else to go. Or they stay because they've gotten used to it and feel safe there.

"Many of the people stay in their rooms and don't say much to anyone. One day I started talking to a guy who always kept to himself. People took advantage of him, took his crack. He didn't even know how much money he was supposed to get

from his case manager. Sometimes I got high with him. And he took a liking to me. When I was getting ready to leave the hotel and told him, I saw his eyes getting wet. I asked him, 'Don, you all right?' He said to me, 'You're my only friend.'

"I met up with Linda in 2001. I had been seeing girls only for sex, but this one girl, I kinda liked, and she kinda stuck around a while. I couldn't get rid of her. So we hooked up. When I couldn't stand the Mission anymore, I went to live with her, but it was difficult. She wanted me to live her way—in her apartment, spending the whole day in front of the TV, drinking beer and smoking. She kept pressuring me and trying to control me. I began getting depressed and started losing interest in her. When I started spending more time on my own, she started denying me sex. Then I really lost interest. We men, we very simple, very easy to placate. Fuck us, feed us, don't mess with our minds, and we cool. We can last a long time on that diet. One day I upped and left and have been living on the streets since then.

"Being on the streets is the thing that helps me with my depression. It's the only place I don't have any obligations to anyone. All I got to do on the streets is take care of myself. I can get high when I want, drunk when I want, talk to whoever I want. It's all for me. No one expects me to give them anything. It's the only way I can keep what I have. When I'm anywhere else, people always want something from me.

"Everyone says how tough it is to be homeless, but I've done this before. I'm good at it. I'm used to it. I know how to survive it. Since I've been outside, I lost 30 pounds, my diabetes and hypertension are under control, I'm stronger, and even my

arthritis is better. Being on the streets is good for my health. Crazy, ain't it?

"Sometimes I sleep in a shelter, in a chair all night, because there's usually no empty beds. I do it for two to three days max, and then if I can't get into a bed after that, I get me some ground cover like a cardboard box and find me a cubbyhole, and sleep there. Otherwise, I get on the subway and ride for five or six hours. Even though I'm sitting up, I can sleep because the rail sound is soothing. One night I was on the train for seven hours, back and forth, back and forth.

"People who have to use the bathroom on the subway, they outta luck. They closed all the subway bathrooms since 911. So people have to pee where they can. I was on the subway once, I peed on the station wall. There was nowhere else to do it. What was I going to do?

"The reason I was late meeting you today is that I had to change my clothes. I was in the subway, and I just couldn't hold it anymore. I was running up the escalator to go to the public bathroom outside, and I started peeing in my pants. It was humiliating.

"San Francisco can get cold. Even though other places like San Diego is warmer, the police there are tougher, not very tolerant of the homeless. They ran them all out. Even in San Francisco, in Mayor Frank Jordan's time, they tried to outlaw homelessness, tried to ship us all out. Made it illegal to be homeless. Can you believe that? If it's illegal to be homeless, give 'em a home. You homeless, you go to jail. That's your new home. Crazy laws. Frank Jordan was a nut.

"The city's new policy of Care Not Cash started out with a big bang because the city had empty rooms to give people in exchange for their welfare checks. Now the rooms are drying up, so people have to give their money to the city, $360 of the $425, just to live in a shelter, on a cot for nine months until a room opens up. The same people who used to be staying in the shelter for free now have to pay for it. They don't want that.

"And shelters are not much better than the streets. The staff who work in the shelters have no real training. They're just doing a low-paying job. The people who need a bed in a shelter have sunk really low in their lives. In order to help them turn their lives around, you have to be able to touch them, and in order to touch them, you have to have some kind of training to recognize when they're hurting. A lot of these people, when they're hurting, automatically go into their 'big bad motherfucker' mode. But the staff don't seem to understand it. All they can see is their attitude, and they say, 'Well, you gotta get outta here. You can't bring that attitude in here.' This 'fuck you' attitude is just hurt, plain and simple. And a lot of the people who use that attitude actually prefer that you get tough with them, because that's what they're used to, that's what they're expecting, that's what they know how to deal with. 'Throw me out, I don't give a fuck!'

"The so-called 'support hotels,' the hotels with social workers, are even worse than the shelters in some ways, because the social workers at least have some training and ought to know better. But they don't do anything. I always wonder why they ain't helping the clients. They see someone needs shoes, why they ain't bringing them to Salvation Army to get shoes? They see people who are reclusive, why they ain't saying, 'Hey, let's get some coffee together'? It's the social worker gotta make the move. You can't expect the client to do it. If the client could, he wouldn't be there in the first place.

"Once I made $10 selling my blood for a diabetes study at the hospital. I used it to by drugs, but the two guys who sold them to me gave me bad stuff. I came back and they were still standing there, like 'Fuck you! We're not afraid of you!' I stabbed one of them in the side and cut off the other one's pinky finger. Another time, I bit a guy's cheek off because he tried to rob me, and I didn't even have any money. I always carry this—a jawbreaker, golf ball in a sock. Hit someone under the chin will break a jaw. My mama would be proud if she were alive.

"She passed away in '92. Been gone a while. I miss her. She was my best friend. She was a bitty thing, 5'2". But she was real tough, mean also. My father was tall, 6'4". When I was a kid, I heard them arguing one day. I came runnin' down the stairs to help my mama, just in time to see my stepfather going through the plate-glass window and then over the hedge, drapes and all. That's what saved him—the drapes wrapped around him. It was my dad I needed to help, not my mama.

"One time she shot him. He had other kids before they were married. His oldest daughter come over one day and got to arguing with my mama. My mama pulled out a pistol and shot at her twice. My daddy jumped in front of her, and he took two bullets in the chest. Now you know what kinda mean she was. He was a big man, but he had to go to the hospital.

"Funny, she wasn't mean to me. I was her favorite. I was the good son. I was a straight-A student. I never gave her any problems at all. I was student body president, athlete, on the chess club, all that. I had a job after school, I cut lawns, I made me a little money. I didn't become a problem until I was 30. And then I started getting a little wild. I never got arrested, though, until I was 32. But I've been arrested three times in the last year, selling drugs, selling crack. I was picked up by an undercover cop. I was in jail for 20 days, was let out, and was back two hours later for selling again.

"People say, 'Well, why do people around here sell drugs? Why don't they work?' But selling is their work, and it's good work. The amount of money you can make in a low-end job like McDonald's is trivial compared to what you can make selling drugs. There are very smart people around here who maybe graduated high school, maybe didn't. But they don't have a skill and can't get a reasonable paying job. In the 'hood, people have no respect for someone who's working at a low-paid job. People get on your case, you're working at McDonald's. It means you don't have any balls, no initiative. Young people in some dead-end job working under a boss eight hours a day see other people working for themselves selling drugs three hours a day, and they say, 'That could be me.' And then they start working the street. But then the street takes them and keeps them.

"But you get jailed even for possession in this state. It's ridiculous. People who are using are just victimizing themselves. It would be like putting someone in jail for not taking his insulin. It costs the government unbelievable amounts of wasted money.

"At one time, they used to call crack 'nigger rocks' 'cause it was so cheap that it was the only form of cocaine that blacks could afford. Asians, whites, they ignored it, they didn't use crack. Now you see even white guys walking down the street buying. It's easy to tell because they have the same look—a slow walk, they're lookin' at everybody, they have a big jacket. They're selling. And nobody has a territory here. Anybody can sell. It's a free-for-all. It's free ball.

"Crack has destroyed the black population, set it against itself, brought it down. Crack is one drug that kinda hypnotizes you when you first use it. It feels so good and it's so highly addictive that all you want to do is keep getting high in your room. A crack high comes and goes in 30 seconds, and then you immediately get a longing for more. You get trapped. You're finished. A lot of men don't even want to be bothered with sex anymore. Women, on the other hand, seem to have better sex on crack. That's one reason why women who use crack tend to lose their morals. They're called toss-ups—women who give sexual favors for crack. Often only for $5—a 'nickel.' So they get two things: crack and good sex.

"I don't think people are ever goin' to stop using and selling if they don't have a better option. Now their only option is jail. Now people say, 'I'd rather use and take the chance on goin' to jail.' Jail, losing their so-called freedom, is nothing to a lot of these people. No big deal, because their freedom ain't worth much of anything. It doesn't really give them anything. They're unemployed and not goin' anyplace in life. They're marking time. And many don't expect to live very long. For some of them, jail is actually a relief for a while. They get a roof over their heads, food. They can clean up, and get their health back if they been strung out. Jail lets them live a while longer, go back on the streets, and because they have no place else to go, *and nothing else to do, they start using again within hours. It's depressing. Everywhere they go, everybody they know is using. It's their life, it's their friends, it's what they know how to do.*

"If the city really wanted to do something to help them, it's gotta do something other than put 'em back on the street, give 'em a welfare check, and expect them to use it to pay for a shitty, overpriced, depressing little room. People would rather live on the streets, smoke crack, and take their chances on getting arrested again. You gotta give 'em something they view as too valuable to lose if they get caught again, like real housing.

"I was the only black working for Bechtel once. I was a draftsman, working on a board. They hired me because they didn't have nobody else at the time, even though I hadn't gone to school for drafting. They had to hire a black. The first job they gave me was designing toilets. When they realized I was good, they gave me a top job, but nobody talked to me after work or during lunch. They'd go for a drink after work, and didn't invite me. They had a bowling league. They didn't ask me to be on it. I felt lonely and hurt and cut out. I got mad, missed work a couple of times, and they put me on probation. But another guy was missing work, they didn't put him on probation. They gave me the hardest jobs at the worst salary, and that's when I snapped. I asked them, 'How come I'm not invited to the bowling league, how come I have to eat lunch all by myself, how come nobody talks to me, how come I always get the hard jobs? I been here three years. Why do you have me training a guy who just came out of college and he's already making more money than me? He's being paid $2,400 a month. I'm getting paid $600 a month. Why?' They had an award ceremony one year and gave a guy

a free three-day trip to Las Vegas for being the top salesman. And I said, 'I'm going to win that next year.' Next year, I made $3 million for the company. Did I get a trip? No fucking way. I got a plaque. Come on!

"You doin' a good project. Just get out there and talk to people. Some people may want money, they poor, they're out there hustling, but some will talk to you even for no money. Many are lonely and just want to talk to someone. Some want to talk because they feel invisible. It's like, 'I'm here.'"

Two months later, Vince left a message on my answering machine telling me that he was going to the hospital to get detoxed from drugs. He'd been having more problems on drugs than he'd been acknowledging to himself or me.

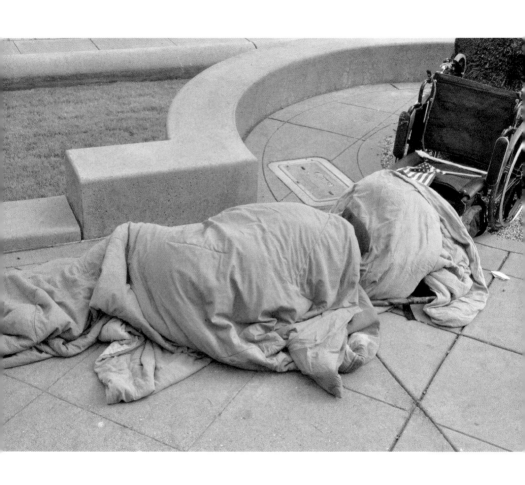

"I WAS LIKE A WOLF. I'D ONLY COME OUT AT NIGHT."

—DON

"I'm the assistant manager of a soup kitchen now, but I'll never, ever forget what kind of life I came from. For over 10 years, I was a drunken bum, living in a campsite along the railroad tracks. Usually, I'd beg for food or eat out of dumpsters. Other times, I'd scrounge for bottles and cans and sell them for 5 cents each to a recycling center. I was like a wolf. I'd only come out at night. I was a recluse. I had a tent, a sleeping bag, and some clothes.

"Before I became a drunk I was happily married, had kids, and earned a good living. But then my wife developed stomach cancer and died. I didn't want to live after that. I was a mess—depressed, crying all the time. Life was a prison of loneliness and missing her. A few months later I began drinking, went through all my money. My wife's treatment had taken most of my money, and alcohol polished the rest off. One night I sat down on a street corner and realized, 'You've got nowhere to go. Man, you're homeless.' I camped under a bridge that night. In the beginning, I was scared stiff I'd be killed. You know, I had read articles in the newspaper about homeless alcoholics being murdered.

"My life was a mess for years until someone told me about this kitchen. When I first came here, I felt as small as a crumb. But the people here took me in without ever putting me down, and slowly I was able to stop drinking, began volunteering here, and reconnected with my family. Four years ago, I became a paid staff member, and a little while later, I was made assistant manager.

"I'd be dead if it weren't for this place."

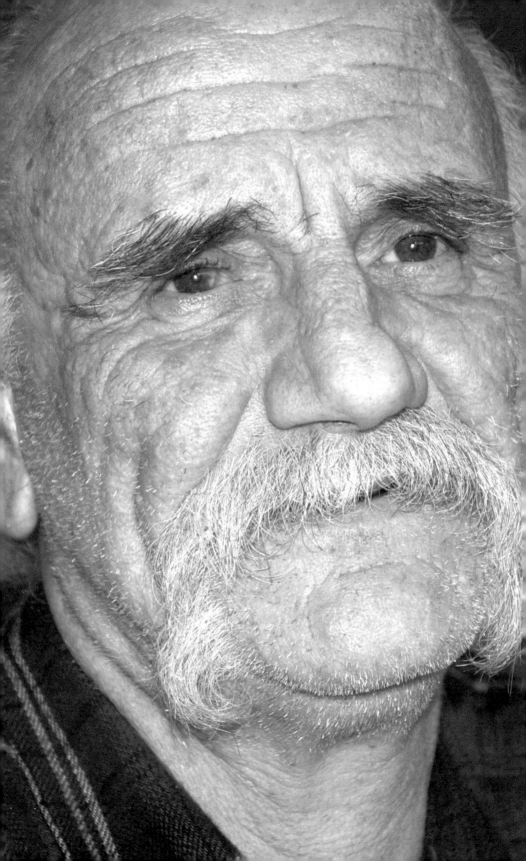

"SOME DAYS, I WAKE UP NOT KNOWING WHO I AM."

—George

"I've had multiple sclerosis since I was 10. I have had some very dramatic episodes. My body has shut down to the point where I can't breathe and I can't swallow. It is terrifying. If it gets too warm, my temperature will go up, like a lizard's. I've been in the hospital the better part of the last two years. They stuck a pacemaker in me.

"They had me on steroids, which was supposed to help my multiple sclerosis, but the steroids gave me osteoporosis, which fractured my hip, and I've been stuck in a wheelchair since then.

"The disease takes away my memory sometimes. Some days, I wake up not knowing who I am. I'm a different character from day to day.

"I've lived a very interrupted life. I'm the only one who's lasted this long with such a bad case of this disease. The most common way that people die with multiple sclerosis is by suicide. They just can't stand the ups and downs, never knowing what part of their bodies are going to go next.

"For a long time, I was a very dangerous person physically. I was what they call a penetration and negotiation specialist for the government. I talked to the Irish Republican Army. I helped make the deal that shut it down. And in return, the government cut me a whole lot of slack when I was caught not having paid $3 million in taxes.

"We burned money as part of the protests against the Vietnam War. Money is nothing. It's no good. It's just paper. We shut down Washington, DC, in 1967. We stopped all the traffic so no one could go to work. I once got sentenced, but the government let me go. I knew too much."

He strummed his guitar for a few minutes and then told me he wanted to go outside for a smoke.

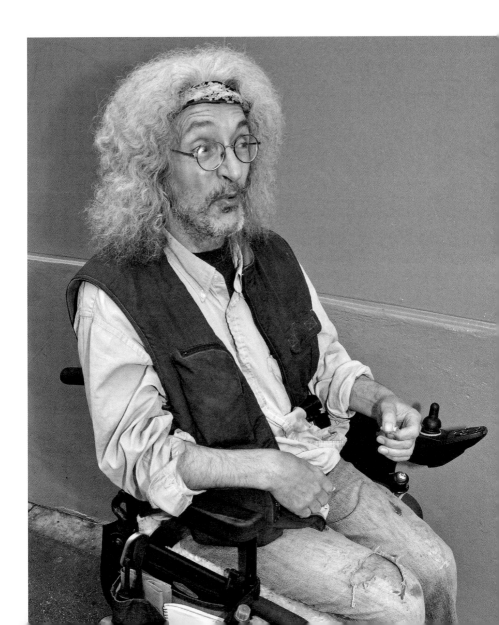

"I WON'T TOUCH THE DEAD BRANCHES OF YOUR FILTH."

—KLAUSS

I met this man in the park near the Ferry Building. He was sitting on a bench talking to himself with an angry intensity. When I approached him, he said, *"You're a murderer in my park and you will be prosecuted in my park. I'm telling you I don't want to hear your shit. And also Herpes, dead lobby ways. I don't want to hear your shit no more. I'm Steven Towndum, the guy who owns the city. He's gone to another place. Queer is where he represents."*

I asked him where he slept last night. *"In this piece of shit,"* he replied.

I asked him where he ate. *"I butt it with a piece of America. I wire food stamps from Bank of America. Some nigger doing her. I won't touch the dead branches of your filth."*

"THEN IN A MATTER OF 2001, ONE OF THESE LITTLE HELICOPTERS CAME DOWN AND SHOT ME IN THE BUTT WITH A BEANGUN." —ROBERT

"I have such an earnest world to live in. I have to look on. Eyes in the back of the head. Supposed to be productivity, but what is productivity? There's the idea that I need a brown eye and a de-browning.

"Have you ever been in a place and someone accosts you? I was wondering whether you had been repetitively set up by somebody who hits you. I did. I got six of them. Just recently out front here, someone came over and hit me aside the head. Just run over and hit me—repetitive the fellow jumped me violently out there—like a compliment, like a helicopter.

"I sleep beneath the overpass. But about three days ago it was during the daytime, you pass underneath the concrete was productive, and to pass out from underneath the concrete within just a matter of moments it was a feeling of lethargy. I had this dell system, a pack of little helicopters, put it through about a year ago. Three small ones and then like a round spinner machine, that's what it looked like. They have these like guns inside the two of them and about a dozen people originally picked me off. They fly up and they fly down. Then in a matter of 2001, one of these came down and shot me in the butt with a beangun and I declined going to anyone about it, at least machine going about it, because a machine shoots like that. But then within four months it shoots on the other side and maybe four months later they shoot in the shoulder and the fewpack

waits around. Out of four of these available, it shot me in the middle of the back here, almost killed me. I laid over there and pretended to pass on, but there somehow muzzled off in the left side of the rear end. It's like a laser atrocity."

CAUSES OF CHRONIC HOMELESSNESS

Even the most cursory examination of the history of the mentally ill reveals that the ebb and flow of contradictory and warring impulses toward these people has been an enduring part of the American landscape for centuries: impulses to help and hurt, treat and mistreat, include and exclude. At different moments in our national history, one or the other of these forces has predominated. But even when prospects for fundamental reform appeared hopeful, even when public policy was primarily animated by therapeutic aspirations, the social stigma associated with mental disorders often acted as a hindrance to the actual implementation of these aims. The darker sentiments evoked by mental disorders that lay hidden, unacknowledged, and unexpressed within the social fabric would then unexpectedly rise to the surface and hijack or weaken the efforts of reform. The resulting compromise would bear only a dim resemblance to advocates' original intentions. Over time, as problems inherent in these half measures became visible, distasteful, or politically unpopular, a new and hopeful wave of reform would arise, only to be weakened by another undertow of resistance. Modern-day homelessness among people with mental illness represents one of the darker tides of this history.

Mental Hospitals: Paving the Way to Homelessness

The people represented in this book are the products of the struggle between opposing forces, described above. The history of these people can be traced back to the beginning of our nation's history.

EMERGENCE OF THE ASYLUM

During the eighteenth and early nineteenth centuries, people with mental disorders who could not be cared for by their families or communities often ended up in almshouses or imprisoned in jails.

In these settings, they were frequently chained naked in cages, stalls, and pens; beaten with rods; lashed into obedience; and preyed on by other residents. Horrified by these grim conditions, the social activist Dorothea Dix, in the second quarter of the nineteenth century, successfully lobbied state legislatures to create asylums for the protection and treatment of people with mental disorders. At the outset, these public asylums were small, well-staffed hospitals that operated under the auspices of state governments and provided so-called moral therapy, a kind of supportive, exhortative treatment based on the theory that mental disorders could be cured by caring staff in a stress-free environment. Many patients after a relatively short period of hospitalization were able to return to their families and communities in a considerably improved state (Ray & Gosling, 1982).

Although the primary impetus behind the establishment of the asylums was benevolent, these facilities also served the less explicit but darker aim of isolating and segregating mentally ill people from the rest of society. Partially to satisfy these latter motivations and partially to achieve economic efficiencies, each hospital functioned like a walled medieval city, completely self-sufficient, with its own forest for lumber and firewood, its own farm animals and vegetable gardens for food, and its own laundry and kitchen. The success of this infrastructure depended on the unpaid labor—one might say slave labor—of the more functional patients, who worked as lumberjacks, farmers, laundresses, maids, and cooks. People who entered these asylums paid a high price for their protection and treatment: isolation from society and the requirement of "work therapy."

DETERIORATION OF THE ASYLUMS

After the Civil War, large waves of immigration, the economic recession of the 1870s, and other engines of social displacement combined to flood state hospitals with many more patients than they could handle. High admission rates in the face of limited staffing transformed these small, relatively humane asylums into large, understaffed, custodial institutions. In exchange for food, clothing, and shelter, patients became anonymous inmates who were provided almost no treatment and had no civil rights, autonomy, privacy, personal possessions, or connection to their families or communities (Ray & Gosling, 1982).

These conditions led to a vicious cycle of longer lengths of stay, larger patient populations, even less treatment, and, in turn, even longer lengths of stay. Many patients who, in a previous era, would have been treated successfully and discharged became "incurable" and were transformed into lifelong institutionalized residents under these adverse conditions. The sense of therapeutic pessimism engendered by this situation became a self-fulfilling prophecy. State governments seized on it as an excuse to justify their unwillingness to provide adequate funding. They could now conveniently argue, "Why provide funds for treatment when the entire venture is hopeless?" Legislators were somehow able to duck the fact that the reason for its hopelessness could be found in their own actions and decisions.

The result of this complete neglect was that by the early 1900s, these institutions became large dumping grounds used by states for the social exclusion, social control, and social welfare of a broad swath of the population who were suffering from mental disorders, alcoholism, intellectual disabilities, epilepsy, neurosyphilis, and various forms of dementia. They also housed many individuals who were simply elderly and infirm, who lacked a source of social or economic support, or who were unacceptably deviant for other reasons. By the mid-twentieth century, the unacknowledged impulses that had contributed to the creation of these facilities in the first place became their predominant function: the lifelong segregation of social rejects.

Given the deterioration in the conditions and reputation of state hospitals, coercion might have inevitably become their primary means of patient admission. Involuntary commitment generally took place without explicit standards and through no formal legal procedure. Moreover, independent judicial reviews of patients' continuing commitment didn't occur. Once people were locked inside the hospital, they often had no way out. State hospitals became prisons for people who had committed no crime.

In summary, within one hundred years, almost every characteristic of state hospitals had been transformed: their size, staffing, and treatment culture; patients' primary legal status, clinical characteristics, and length of stay; and the functions that society expected of them.

DEINSTITUTIONALIZATION

By 1955, the population of state hospitals had climbed to 560,000 (Ray & Gosling, 1982). At this time, the anesthetic chlorpromazine was serendipitously discovered. Later branded as Thorazine, this drug could ameliorate the psychotic symptoms of certain patients, even some who had been considered completely hopeless. For the first time, more patients were discharged from than admitted to state hospitals. The process of deinstitutionalization had begun.

Consisting of the large-scale discharge of patients from state hospitals and a restriction in the number of new admissions, the policy and process of deinstitutionalization quickly steamrolled across the country. One of the important reasons for its widespread adoption was its broad appeal to parts of society that were generally on opposite sides of the political spectrum.

State governments supported deinstitutionalization as a way of reining in the growing costs of public hospitalization. Civil rights attorneys seized on it as a way of eliminating an abusive deprivation of liberty. Mental health professionals promoted it as a way of freeing up money from a failed institutional system to fund a modern community treatment system. Of these three groups, state governments had the most power and influence on the process.

The political alliance among these groups ultimately broke down when it became clear that the savings that had been anticipated from reduced state hospital populations were not materializing because the fixed costs of caring for the remaining clients continued to be high. Those savings that could be realized were absorbed by state governments rather than reallocated to create community services. In defense of this policy, state governments argued that they were no longer responsible for caring for patients once they had been discharged. This stance was viewed by mental health professionals and advocates for the mentally ill as a deep betrayal since their support for deinstitutionalization had been predicated on the promise that funding would follow patients out of the hospital and into the community. The result of the process of deinstitutionalization was that large numbers of incredibly vulnerable patients were pushed out of institutions onto the streets with no real plan to help them, and the door locked behind them. While those who were more functional flourished simply by being freed from an adverse environment, many less functional people suffered greatly and found themselves as isolated and poor in their new communities as they had been in their old state hospitals. As a result of aggressive discharge and restrictive admission policies, the state hospital population in the United States declined from 560,000 in 1950 to 38,000 in 2016 (Treatment Advocacy Center, 2016b). Lacking a place to live and with no support, many people had nowhere to go but the streets. Before long and without services, the number of visible casualties in cities and towns began to mount.

The Drug Epidemic

Community life was bound to be difficult for people who had spent years segregated from it, but the drug epidemic that developed in the 1970s and continues to this day made the situation infinitely worse. It transformed the face of mental disorders and altered the course of deinstitutionalization in the United States. A high proportion of patients who were initially treated with psychiatric medications found the side effects intolerable and were constantly reminded by these side effects that they were "crazy" and would be so until the day they died. Many turned to street drugs as a physically and emotionally more comforting way to alter their states of consciousness and dull their emotional pain. Before long, many people with mental illness were also suffering from drug addiction (National Institute of Drug Abuse, 2021).

While affording temporary subjective relief to many people, street drugs rendered the intrinsically complex problems of mental disorders even more destructive, intransigent, and difficult to treat. These drugs frequently aggravated patients' psychiatric symptoms, further compromised their diminished sense of reality and impulse control, and weakened their motivation for treatment. They also increased their vulnerability to predators on the street, involved them in criminal activities, pushed them into the arms of the correctional system, and increased their risk of dying from drug-related complications. Drugs, mental disorders, homelessness, and incarceration became a vicious cycle from which many never escaped.

THE FEDERAL RESPONSE— TOO LITTLE, TOO LATE

While patients were living in mental hospitals operated by state governments, the problems of the mentally ill had historically been defined as a state responsibility. But once these patients were discharged, as mentioned earlier, states tried to divest themselves of responsibility for them. The federal government, in turn, argued that the care of the mentally ill had always been the responsibility of the states, one that they could not shirk even after patients had left their mental hospitals. These opposing views resulted in a standoff that continued until the early 1960s, when the federal government, responding to the large number of poor untreated patients in communities across the country, could no longer ignore them. In 1963, eight years after the beginning of deinstitutionalization, Congress, under the leadership of President Kennedy, enacted the Community Mental Health Act. The explicit intent of the centers that this act established was to treat patients who had been discharged from state hospitals.

Unfortunately, this act ended up failing the very patients it was created to serve. In the first place, it was never funded sufficiently to establish community mental health centers in all areas of the United States. Second, the centers, contrary to their original intent, found it almost irresistible to treat a relatively healthy population rather than people who had been discharged from state hospitals. The latter, which should have constituted the majority of their caseloads, represented only 4 to 7 percent. Third, despite its original mandate, the community mental health center legislation failed to include in its provisions for funding some of the essential services that disabled people needed to survive in the community. Rehabilitative services, housing, linkage to jobs, and case management services were never provided by the centers until relatively late in the deinstitutionalization process.

Contributing to the abandonment of seriously mentally ill patients and undermining even the small efforts that the community mental health centers made on their behalf was the failure of the federal government to establish an infrastructure to support these efforts. The so-called safety net that the government finally created—which included Supplemental Security Income (SSI), Medicaid, Medicare, and housing subsidies—was grossly underfunded and virtually guaranteed that the mentally ill in the United States would be forced to subsist under conditions found in developing countries. The SSI stipends, on which people with serious mental illness depended for their rent, food, and other expenses, were set so low as to ensure these individuals would live out their lives in abject poverty. Medicaid and Medicare, while providing important physical and mental health benefits, were also far from robust in the services they reimbursed, with the result that the treatment severely mentally ill people received was limited in amount, scope, relevance, and number of people covered. Although health insurance legislation, such as the Affordable Care Act (a.k.a. Obamacare), was finally enacted to provide reimbursement to a large part of the poor population, it is currently in constant danger of being dismantled. Legislation designed to provide rental assistance to people in imminent danger of losing their housing and to help people get off the streets was, and has always been, funded at such a low level as to guarantee that homelessness would become an ongoing feature of the American landscape. These subsidies, in fact, are available to only 10 percent of the people who need it.

It is crucially important to recognize that the inadequacies of the social "safety" net are not an accident. They are not due to poor planning or an inability of the government to predict their inevitable consequences. Notwithstanding the huge amount of wealth that exists in this society, these inadequacies are built into the system's very design, the result of a collective decision that poor people, particularly those who are homeless or in danger of becoming so, are entitled to only a negligible amount of society's prosperity. Although government actions are the proximate cause of this, Washington is simply carrying out the wishes of its citizens. The government may be *making* the decisions that keep people impoverished, but we, through our silence, are *endorsing* these decisions. Largely unmentioned in discussions of homelessness is ironically one of its most important underlying causes—the large disparities in wealth that are built into the fabric of our society and the government decisions that help create and perpetuate these disparities. As I discuss later, it is mostly these disparities that create such a large group of very poor homeless people at the lower end of the economic spectrum and that make the creation of a safety net necessary in the first place. Even when we recognize the existence of these disparities, we don't connect them with the problem of homelessness and don't question whether the system is fair or just but accept it as a normal and natural fact of our economic life—as American as apple pie. It would be the unusual citizens who, when asked about the underlying causes of homelessness, would include the inequalities of wealth and the government's ongoing role in perpetuating it. And even if they did, would they endorse its obvious implications: that the economic structure of this society must be modified and government policies dramatically reformed to mitigate these inequalities and the desperate poverty and homelessness that flow from them?

COMMUNITY MENTAL HEALTH— POORLY CONCEIVED, POORLY FUNDED

It was not until the 1980s, and only after thousands of patients had been discharged, that community mental health programs began to develop services more relevant to the survival needs of disabled patients. Most important of these were case management services. Case managers were tasked with helping people find housing and apply for the limited government benefits that were available and teaching them how to shop, launder their clothes, use transportation, protect their meager resources, take their medications, and manage their symptoms. As crucial as they were to patients' survival, however, case management services were never sufficiently funded. Clinicians, burdened by unrealistically high caseloads, found themselves completely overwhelmed by clients with multiple and complex medical, psychiatric, social, and economic problems and without a broader social and economic infrastructure necessary to support their work. Staff were able to spend only a limited amount of time with each client. Job satisfaction was low, staff burnout and turnover was high. Clients were handed successively from one clinician to another, rarely having the opportunity to develop the kind of long-term stable relationships they could trust and depend on. Many of the less functional and more complex clients, without adequate case management support, were unable to maintain themselves in even the most primitive form of housing—SRO hotels—and often drifted to the streets as a result.

In addition to the resource-driven limitations on the time clinicians could spend with clients, and in the absence of a robust social safety net that could have helped them support their clients' needs for food and shelter, staff were also constrained by the narrow clinical model within which they were forced to work and the fee-for-service reimbursement system that financed it. This narrow paradigm, which had destroyed peoples' souls in state hospitals and had always been limited to addressing their most basic physical needs and psychiatric symptoms, was largely transferred to the new community system with an equally limited vision. This model tended to medicalize peoples' suffering and led to staff missing the other causes of their distress: their poverty, isolation, exclusion from the fabric of society, social and economic problems, lack of meaning, and segregation in the vocational, social, and political realms. And even if they recognized them as problems in theory, case managers lacked the resources and time to address them.

Although a more progressive model of rehabilitation with higher aspirations and a broader vision emerged at the end of the twentieth century, it was given only lip service by the government. Service providers often adopted the rehabilitation model in name only for no real funding structure existed to support and realistically implement it in practice. Services still had to be deemed "medically necessary," which made it almost inevitable that staff would continue to see their clients through the restricted lens of their symptoms and diagnoses. Simply as a matter of self-preservation and to spare themselves overwhelming frustration, staff had to limit their aspirations to those interventions that fit into the narrow strictures of this model since the system of reimbursement available to them wouldn't pay for anything else. Clinicians had almost no time, and certainly not the mandate, to help clients deal with other aspects of their lives—how to manage their meager resources, develop vocational skills so they could find a job, cultivate friendships, spend their leisure time, create a sense of meaning in their lives, and envision a future that involved anything more than how to scrape by and meet their most basic needs for survival.

Symptomatic of the limits that the system placed on both staff and clients was a completely self-defeating practice that developed in many mental health systems. As soon as clients had made even a small amount of progress in achieving the limited goals that staff had set for them, they were deemed to no longer need that level of service and were relegated to a lower level with less staff attention so that room could be made for other more disturbed clients. This guaranteed a ceiling on their futures that limited their capacities and aspirations and kept their lives empty. The system entitled them to nothing more.

The Emergence and Deficiencies of the General Hospital

During the same time that community mental health centers were struggling to care for a more difficult patient population, other parts of the health-care system were gaining an increasing share of society's resources. General medical hospitals expanded as a result of acute treatment modalities that required overnight stays for patients with physical problems. But before long, with the advent of improved medical technology, the length of stay for medical and surgical patients began to decline. This led to an increase in the number of empty beds, a trend that presented these hospitals with a need for a new cohort of patients. Psychiatric patients, whose treatment was increasingly being reimbursed by the private and public sectors, were obvious candidates to fill this niche and quickly became its beneficiaries. Within fifty years, general hospitals converted many of their empty medical and surgical beds into psychiatric beds within small twenty-patient units. By 1998 the number of psychiatric patients in general hospitals grew from almost zero to 54,434. Inpatient beds in private psychiatric hospitals also increased from 14,229 in 1970 to a high of 45,000 before dropping back to 25,095 in 2002 (Lipsitt, 2003). Most patients who needed hospitalization and who previously had been admitted to large state hospitals were admitted, instead, to general hospital psychiatric units and to private psychiatric hospitals.

While in no way offsetting the dramatic decrease in state hospital beds, the use of general hospitals for psychiatric patients represented a real improvement for those who could gain admission.

Many patients needing psychiatric treatment could be cared for in their local communities, where families could visit them and from which planning for their aftercare was logistically easier. The integration of psychiatric patients into general community medical hospitals also reduced some of the stigma associated with mental disorders by medicalizing their image. Psychiatric units in general hospitals were required by hospital-accrediting organizations to meet the more exacting staffing and treatment standards that had, for a long time, exclusively protected physically ill patients but had not been required for psychiatric patients in mental hospitals. The increased quality of care also made it easier to attract high-quality medical, nursing, and social work staff than it had been in mental hospitals. In summary, the inclusion of psychiatric patients into general hospitals brought inpatient psychiatric care into the mainstream of modern medicine.

Over time, private and public funding organizations, faced with increasing budget restrictions, became less willing to pay for the relatively long lengths of stay that had become typical for psychiatric units. As a result, general hospitals decreased the length of time they were willing to provide care—from an average of thirty days to seven days (Lipsitt, 2003). The most important cause of this was a change in the way federal and state governments interpreted the Medicaid law, which specified that patients' conditions meet a standard of medical necessity as the criteria for reimbursement. By then narrowing the definition of medical necessity to exclude all but those patients who met the very strict criteria for involuntary admission, federal and state governments, using their power of the purse, effectively pressured hospitals into refusing to admit many very sick psychiatric patients who were voluntarily willing to admit themselves and prematurely discharging patients who had been admitted as soon as they were no longer dangerous. Many were pushed out the door before their symptoms could be stabilized and before they could be linked to housing or even shelters.

To accommodate the unrealistic discharge requirements of Medicaid, and in the absence of alternatives, hospitals came to view the streets as an acceptable discharge option. Unsurprisingly, many patients were forced to return for further care. The revolving door of readmissions in and out of hospitals became a common phenomenon in many cities, as was evidenced by the 22.4 percent readmission rate of patients with schizophrenia in less than thirty days (Heslin & Weiss, 2015). Other patients who were prematurely discharged to the streets simply languished there.

The federal government often touts its efforts to ameliorate the problem of homelessness, which makes its very restrictive interpretation of Medicaid regulations particularly ironic. At the same time one part of the federal government (i.e., the Department of Housing and Urban Development) makes certain efforts, though grossly insufficient, to reduce the homeless problem, another part of the government (i.e., the Department of Health and Human Services) and its state partners seem intent on pursuing policies whose only possible outcome is to increase it.

THE TILT TO CIVIL LIBERTIES

Another phenomenon that amplified the barriers to acute care in general hospitals and led to a growing number of untreated patients in the community was the enactment of more rigorous state commitment legislation. These laws made it more difficult to commit patients to hospitals and restricted the time they could be confined there even if funding was available to pay for them in certain cases. Physicians were required to substantiate with hard behavioral evidence that patients with mental illness were an imminent danger to themselves or others or were so gravely disabled that they were unable to meet their basic needs for food, shelter, and safety. This legislation was designed to correct the practice of committing people without cause and was successful in doing so but sometimes at the expense of their mental health. Courts that were empowered to interpret this legislation went overboard in their attempt to protect peoples' civil liberties. They began to restrict the criteria for grave disability in order to "liberate" patients from hospitals even if they were severely psychotic and had no home to return to, no alternative form of shelter, and no food available except what they could scrounge from garbage cans and bins (Torrey, n.d.). As long as they could survive on the streets, with or without shelter, however tenuously, and no matter how much their health was imperiled, courts too often refused to commit them (Southern California Psychiatric Society, 2021).

Were adequate treatment alternatives available, it would have been possible to treat many of these people on a voluntary outpatient basis without either restricting their liberty through forced hospitalization or abandoning them because they failed to meet the grave disability standard for commitment. But in too many cases, such alternatives were lacking, with the result that patients unreasonably discharged by the courts received no treatment and no housing at all. The consequences of this misguided interpretation of states' commitment legislation can be seen in every large city in America.

CRIMINALIZATION OF THE MENTALLY ILL

Notwithstanding the stated rationale for enacting civil commitment legislation, many people were not spared a restriction of their liberties by the way that this legislation was interpreted by the courts. By denying involuntary hospitalization to people whose capacity to care for themselves was so profoundly impaired, judges often unwittingly consigned mentally ill people to the criminal justice system. Police, frustrated by the refusal or inability of hospitals to admit certain patients, as well as reacting to the restrictive practices of the courts, brought them to jail instead to give these people some type of refuge, however inappropriate. Many patients thus gained their freedom from one institution only to lose it in another, much less benign institution (Lamb & Weinberger, 2005).

The other paths to the criminalization of the mentally ill were much less protective in their intent than that described above. Many cities enacted harsh ordinances against homeless mentally ill people. Sleeping in public places, shoplifting, urinating on the street, or just "acting crazy" were often enough to trigger the arrest of people with mental disorders (Kieschnick, 2018).

This practice of course did nothing to prevent a repetition of the behaviors that were punished since alternative behaviors that stayed clear of antihomelessness ordinances were unrealistic given the realities of life on the streets. Moreover, the practice clogged up the courts and jails, wasted city money, and added stress to the lives of people who were already overwhelmed. Where exactly were homeless people going to lie down if they had no other place to do so than the streets? One is left to wonder exactly what purpose such ordinances were designed to achieve other than to clear the streets of these people and punish them for the inevitable consequences of being homeless in the first place.

Back-door violations of patients' civil rights were not the only consequence of the shift from hospitals to jails. The mental disorders that led to their arrests in the first place were often aggravated by the crowded, dangerous, and punitive conditions of many correctional institutions. People with mental disorders frequently became targets of abuse by other inmates. Because psychiatric services in most jails were, and continue to be, minimal, these people remained highly symptomatic and were forced to endure prolonged suffering as a result. Incarceration also entailed a loss of their Medicaid and SSI benefits, requiring that they begin the lengthy and complicated process of reinstatement of these benefits all over again at the end of their sentences, a process that often took months. Some people had the ability to do this, others didn't and were consequently poorer and more vulnerable in every respect at the end of their incarceration than before. Finally, jails had a limited capacity to help them prepare for community life after their release. People were typically dumped out of their cells at the end of their jail or prison terms with fifty dollars in their pockets, a single change of clothes, no place to go, no health or welfare benefits, and no link to mental health treatment other than an address or telephone number of some agency scribbled on a scrap of paper.

It is generally agreed that the use of these forensic institutions for people with mental illness is ineffective as a deterrent, wasteful as an economic policy, harmful as a clinical intervention, and offensive to the most elementary sense of justice. Beyond this, the practice of jailing mentally ill people for nuisance crimes, failing to provide adequate treatment when they are incarcerated, and dumping them from jail onto the street once their sentences have been completed with no money, no place to live, and no treatment almost ensures they will circle through a rapidly revolving door to and from the streets, similar to that which has occurred in hospitals (Sentencing Project, 2002). The entire process was, and continues to be, a setup for further deterioration, recidivism, and reincarceration. Moreover, this practice goes on without any public outcry. Perhaps jail is where the public feels these people truly belong. Perhaps their confinement reassures us they cannot hurt us. Perhaps if they are confined to jail, we don't have to see them.

The numbers of mentally ill people in the criminal justice system today are staggering. Some jails now house more mentally ill people than any state or private psychiatric hospital in the country. In 2016, while fewer than 38,000 people were receiving treatment in psychiatric hospitals at any given time, 380,000 mentally ill people, more than ten times that number, were serving time in jails and prisons (Treatment Advocacy Center, 2016a). Studies have demonstrated that 16 to 40 percent of inmates have mental disorders (Torrey, n.d.; Ditton, 1999). In state prisons, 40 percent of white women aged twenty-four and younger are mentally ill. Los Angeles County Jail has become the largest "mental hospital" in the country, incarcerating more mentally ill people than any actual mental hospital (Torrey, n.d.; Butterfield, 1999). The wheel of history that began revolving in the eighteenth and early nineteenth centuries, with mentally ill people housed in jails, had turned a full revolution by 2000. Even considering the overall increase in the population, mentally ill people were back in the correctional system in even greater numbers than they had been before they were transferred to asylums.

THE LACK OF AFFORDABLE HOUSING

The most important cause of chronic homelessness is the lack of affordable housing. As more and more people were discharged into the community from state hospitals and were later refused admission to or prematurely discharged from general hospitals, powerful demographic changes were occurring in various cities that pushed up rents beyond which many people could afford. These changes continued over several decades and have accelerated recently to the point that the most important proximate cause of homelessness in the United States is now the lack of affordable housing. San Francisco is the poster child for these changes and dramatically illustrates them. Between 2009 and 2015, San Francisco added 123,000 new jobs, many high paying, from the relocation of high tech and other companies into the city but added only 11,000 new housing units (Bellisario et al., 2016). Driven by an increased demand and an extremely limited supply, the average monthly rent for one-bedroom apartments in San Francisco rose to $3,363 at a time when Social Security Disability Insurance was paying only $800 a month. Between 2012 and 2017, the median rent in the city skyrocketed by 38 percent from $2,900 to $4,000 (CBS San Francisco, 2021).

The result of these unforgiving changes in the balance of supply and demand was entirely predictable, though city governments encouraged the growth in the urban workforce and thus indirectly contributed to this phenomenon. Poor people living on marginal incomes or vulnerable for other reasons, such as being mentally ill, were squeezed out of their once-affordable apartments into SRO hotels situated in the poorest part of town or onto the streets. In these SRO rooms, usually having no kitchen or private bathrooms, residents with mental illnesses lived alone, impoverished, and cut off from their families with minimal staff supervision and almost no personal possessions. Nothing in their rooms reflected their individual identities. Most lived in these settings for years, subsisting on a level of government support that barely covered the cost of these rooms, much less anything else. Faced with the choice of paying for rent, food, or drugs, some people opted for the latter, often choosing to give up their rooms, no matter how drastic the alternative. Many others couldn't secure even this kind of low-cost dilapidated room. With no right to housing in the United States, the declining number of affordable apartments generated by the process of gentrification, and a change in the balance of supply and demand, many poor people living on marginal incomes or vulnerable for other reasons were pushed out of the housing market altogether and onto the streets.

It is important to emphasize that the drastic changes in the balance between supply and demand of affordable housing didn't just happen. Too often, and despite their public handwringing about the problem of homelessness, governments have sided with big business over poor, disabled people who lack the power to exact a price on politicians at the ballot box and who are thus unable to influence their decisions. City governments, motivated by the promise of increases to their tax base, actually encouraged companies, with their well-paid employees and huge profit margins, to relocate or remain there, offering tax breaks, cash grants, rebates, and other incentives—actions that were bound to distort the balance between supply and demand but completely ignored the obvious and drastic consequences for people just trying to hang on to their low-cost apartments. In the United States, based on the most recent figures, the estimated total annual value of these fiscal incentives was around $90 billion (Parilla & Liu, 2018).

Even when local governments haven't actually enticed companies to relocate, they have often sat by and failed to take action when unregulated market forces have distorted the housing market, driven up rents, and pushed people onto the streets. By declining to exercise their power to prevent such dislocation, governments have contributed, however silently, to the problem of homelessness. An example of this is the case of Blackstone, the largest real estate owner in the world. Blackstone, funded by private equity firms that in turn receive much of their money from pension funds, has generated enormous profits by buying up low-income, distressed properties and after modest improvements, flipping them for much higher rents, which the original tenants could never afford, thus pushing them out of the housing market (Edwards, 2019). Instead of using their power to mitigate this phenomenon of gentrification, many city governments have either encouraged or allowed it to happen.

A specific example of this occurred in New York City, which for years did nothing to oppose the effect of market forces on the gentrification of the low-income housing stock. In fact, the city gave tax breaks to developers who converted SROs into other forms of housing. As a result, between 1955 and 1995, the number of SRO units declined from 200,000 to less than 40,000. Between 1976 and 1981, those incentives resulted in the loss of nearly two-thirds of the SROs in the city. The same process occurred for other low-income units. The result is that as of 2020, there were some 25 million applications submitted for roughly 40,000 units (Jacobs, 2021). Where did the mentally ill people who lived in these low-income dwellings go? Many were forced onto the street.

This and other examples illustrate the close relationship between market forces, government action and inaction, and the problem of homelessness. It also indicates that homelessness isn't exclusively a condition intrinsic to the individual but is also a result of larger social and economic forces that selectively affect the most vulnerable people in society. It moreover reveals that poorly executed deinstitutionalization alone was not the only, or even the primary, cause of modern-day homelessness. Many people who had been discharged from state hospitals lived in SROs until the 1970s, when they were displaced by uncontested market forces. Thus, what may appear to be simply the result of natural market forces are, in fact, often the result of acts of commission and omission by federal, state, and city governments, who are silent coconspirators in the creation of homelessness. It is hard to avoid the conclusion that homelessness is, to some extent, a government-sponsored program.

Certain cities have actually opposed measures that would have provided resources to ameliorate the problem. In 2018, when the voters in San Francisco passed a resolution to levy a 0.5 percent tax on the city's wealthiest businesses with revenues in excess of $50 million, a resolution that would have paid for an additional 4,000 new supported-housing beds and 1,000 new shelter beds, the mayor opposed the resolution on the grounds that it would be bad for business, which even the city's controller sharply contested. Not surprisingly, the measure was fought by the companies in court. Ironically, many of these companies had profited from relocating to San Francisco in the first place and had been responsible for both driving up the cost of housing in the city and pushing more people onto the street. Instead of contributing to the voters' attempt to help the people who had lost their homes, the companies did the opposite and tried to actively thwart these efforts. Fortunately, these companies lost in court, though only on a legal technicality. Finally, and only after several years following the passage of the resolution, the city was able to use the resources enacted by the citizens to begin creating the housing that the proposition intended.

City governments haven't been the only ones to sit on their hands in dealing with the problem of homelessness. At a time when homelessness has reached a national crisis, the federal government, through its Department of Housing and Urban Development (HUD), provides rental assistance to less than half of households that are severely cost burdened (defined as those that spend 50 percent or more of their income on housing) and who are often one paycheck away from losing their housing altogether. According to data from the Census Bureau's American Community Survey, 18.5 million households were severely cost burdened, and 19.6 million households were moderately cost burdened in 2016. In a more optimistic though questionable 2017 report, HUD found that roughly 8.3 million renter households (7 percent of all households) were severely cost burdened. This represented an increase compared to 2013, when 7.7 million renter households (6.7 percent of all households) were severely cost burdened. Between 1987 and 2015, the number of very low-income renters grew by 6 million while the number of those assisted by the federal government grew by only 950,000 (McCarty et al., 2019). The result in a county like Los Angeles, for example, is stark. Roughly one in thirty very poor people who applied for assistance in 2019 actually received a voucher because the demand so greatly exceeded the supply (Editorial Board, 2019). People often have to wait years before their names come to the top of the list for housing assistance.

But even when people are able to obtain housing vouchers, they often face insuperable obstacles to using them. One problem is that the federally determined fair market rent, on which vouchers are based, is often much lower than the level defined by the market that places apartments out of reach and makes the voucher practically unusable. Another problem is that many landlords are unwilling to lease to renters with government vouchers altogether. For example, a HUD-funded study in Los Angeles revealed that 76 percent of the landlords surveyed refused to accept government vouchers. The denial rate was even higher in more affluent communities, where 82 percent of landlords refused to take vouchers (Editorial Board, 2019).

In summary, the number of severely cost-burdened families has grown substantially, and the availability of Section 8 vouchers, which was never adequate to begin with, has failed to keep pace with the growth in the number of these families, leading to a huge and widening disparity between the need and the supply. And even those who are fortunate enough to obtain Section 8 vouchers often find themselves unable to use them. Finally, the paperwork requirements for obtaining vouchers is so complicated that many of those people who arguably need the vouchers most desperately—the mentally ill—are in practice excluded from the voucher program altogether. Many such people simply give up trying to get the limited assistance that is theoretically available and surrender to what seems to them like the inevitability of remaining homeless forever.

Another example of local governments' collusion in either causing or failing to prevent homelessness is its reaction to the not-in-my-backyard (NIMBY) phenomenon (Sentencing Project, 2002). This has been a major problem in developing new housing for homeless mentally ill people. Motivated by fears of declining property values, misplaced anxieties about their safety, beliefs that their neighborhoods will be dirtied, or wishes to avoid having to see homeless mentally ill people altogether, otherwise well-meaning citizens have used their political influence to block the siting of shelters and supported housing "in their backyards." Solutions to the homeless problem are applauded by these citizens, but only if they are implemented somewhere beyond the horizon of their own collective vision. Instead of challenging this phenomenon, governments, responding to their political pressure, have too often colluded by capitulating to it, with the result that such housing has been prevented altogether or is pushed into disadvantaged neighborhoods, already staggering under multiple social burdens of drugs, disability, and poverty.

THE INADEQUACY OF SHELTERS

To save people from the cruelest conditions of the street, many cities began to create temporary shelters. Unfortunately, these settings were often poorly designed, poorly funded, and frequently harsh in other ways. The total number of beds available in many cities usually doesn't come close to meeting the need. In San Francisco, for example, there are 1,200 shelter beds for over 5,000 unsheltered homeless people who are forced to compete for the beds that are available. Until recently, San Francisco made the policy decision to allocate its limited funding primarily for the development of permanent housing to the relative exclusion of shelter beds. In fact, in 2004, the city actually reduced the number of its shelter beds, even though their number at the time was not close to meeting its need. In a three-year period, shelter beds in San Francisco were reduced by over one-third, from 1,910 to 1,203, on the forecast that the city would be able to create 3,000 permanent housing units—a number that was anticipated to eliminate the need for many of these temporary beds (Josefowitz, 2018). This proved to be an expensive gamble on the lives of the most vulnerable people in the city, one that failed to predict the economic dislocation created by the coming tech boom that pushed many of these people out of their low-cost apartments onto the streets. Although the city almost met its permanent housing goal, however inadequate, overall homelessness increased. Instead of a reduction in the unsheltered population, their numbers doubled, leaving 2,655 unhoused people in 2005. In 2019, 5,180 unhoused people were forced to compete for 1,203 shelter beds (City and County of San Francisco, 2020). Like many other cities, San Francisco failed to understand the overwhelming effect of economic factors in determining the extent of homelessness and instead relied on simplistic mathematical models that ignored these circumstances. Even when the consequences of these causes became obvious, cities did little to oppose them.

Beyond their grossly insufficient number, the shelter beds that were created were poorly designed in many cities. Because they lacked the number of beds necessary to serve the need, sleeping spaces were assigned on a first come, first serve basis to people who consequently were forced to stand in line for several hours, often outdoors, before they learned whether a bed was available for them that night. People who didn't make the cut were turned away to sleep on the streets. People who were able to gain entrance were only marginally more fortunate, for they were often stuffed into beds so close together that they were in perpetual danger of contracting each other's contagious diseases. Moreover, people with certain kinds of mental disorders who were particularly frightened of getting too close to other people, either physically or emotionally, couldn't tolerate such intimate sleeping arrangements.

Shelters also often refused admission to people with pets. Many shelters developed the reputation of being poorly supervised and, frankly, dangerous. They often failed to provide locked personal storage space, making everyone's possessions vulnerable to theft. Many people refused to use shelters after repeated experiences of losing what few possessions they had. One of the most disrespectful but common practices of shelters was to turn out their "guests" early in the morning, no matter how inclement the weather. In the afternoon, the process of lining up would begin again. For all these reasons, the shelter system was, and too often continues to be, an unreliable, frustrating, unsafe, punishing, and humiliating experience. Over the years, thousands of people simply gave up on them and decided to take their chances outside in the rough, even though sleeping on the street was grueling, physically demanding, emotionally stressful, demeaning, and dangerous.

ADVERSE CHILDHOOD EVENTS AND THE FAILURES OF THE FOSTER CARE SYSTEM

In the last two decades, it has become increasingly obvious that one of the frequent but hidden causes of homelessness of people with serious mental illness is their history of so-called adverse childhood events, most notably abuse and neglect (Patterson et al., 2014). One study found that 78 percent of women living in temporary shelters reported having been the victim of childhood abuse; of those with an abuse history, 55 percent reported sexual abuse, 67 percent physical abuse, and 90 percent emotional abuse (Anderson et al., 1988). Another study investigated the prevalence of childhood adversity among older homeless adults with mental illness and found that 71 percent reported at least one adverse childhood event and 8.3 percent reported four or more (Lee et al., 2016). The high prevalence of adverse childhood events in the lives of homeless mentally ill women and men were reported in other studies as well. These often included one or more incidents of physical, sexual, or emotional abuse; family breakdown; domestic violence; and parental addiction or mental illness. While we rarely consider this when we pass by homeless adults, these people were once children who came from chaotic or abusive families and were often emotionally and functionally compromised from the earliest years of their lives.

Although sometimes obvious and dramatic in their presentation, the effects of exposure to these families were often not identified in childhood when they could have been treated or ameliorated. These include significant problems in executive functioning, unhealthy coping behaviors and social relationship patterns, poor school performance, difficulty complying with rules, and poor levels of adaptation. Having little or no help, and attempting to deal by themselves with the emotional chaos and traumatic experiences of their families, these children begin to self-medicate with street drugs, run away from home during their teenage years, turn to the paradoxically comforting effects of self-harm and suicide attempts, or engage in violent or criminal behaviors. Their school performance deteriorates due to both the trauma itself and the ways children learn to cope with it. They often enter adulthood with no employable skills, difficult interpersonal relationships, self-defeating behaviors, severe problems organizing their lives, and mental disorders, all of which frequently lead to homelessness. A national survey in Wales found that, compared to those with no experience of adverse childhood events, individuals with four or more such events were sixteen times more likely to have experienced one or more episodes of homelessness in their lives (Grey & Woodfine, 2019). Another survey of homeless adults with mental illness revealed that 50 percent had experienced multiple adverse childhood events: 50 percent had experienced four or more and 19 percent had experienced three (Edalati et al., 2017).

A particularly vulnerable subgroup of children are those who are taken away from their families and placed in foster care or the juvenile justice system. These children have already been identified as coming from destructive households and need intense interventions focused on ameliorating the effects of their adverse experiences. But these systems are hopelessly under-funded and struggle to provide interventions needed by these children. The dimensions of the problem are almost unfathom-able. About 400,000 kids are in foster care at any given time in the United States. If they aren't traumatized before entering foster care, many are after being taken away from their families and placed with strangers who are sometimes just as dysfunc-tional as, if not more so, than the homes from which they were removed and on whom they have to depend.

Many children are moved from foster home to foster home, from school to school, frequently twice a year. Too often, when they show evidence of emotional pain in the form of difficult behaviors, they are medicated rather than given the kind of understanding, support, and counseling that could save them from the effects of their trauma. The impact of these experi-ences is compounded when they age out of the foster care sys-tem at age eighteen and are forced to leave their foster care families. Roughly 4,000 of the 20,000 who age out each year become homeless the day they leave their foster homes. Within eighteen months of emancipation 40 to 50 percent become homeless. Only half of the foster kids who age out of the system will be gainfully employed by age twenty-four, a certain prelude to homelessness for many of them (Dronen, n.d.).

The impact of foster care and the family traumas that necessitate it on the crisis of homelessness is profound. One-half of the adult homeless population was previously in foster care. In a study of 442 homeless adults with mental illness studied in Vancouver, British Columbia, 30 percent were previously in foster care, 38 percent of whom had been placed there because of parental abuse and neglect (Patterson et al., 2014).

How can we let our neglect of these children happen in the richest nation on earth? These youth are not anonymous. We know who they are and that they are at extremely high risk. We know that without intervention many will surely flow into the river of homelessness. And yet we let it happen. When we see a homeless mentally ill person lying on the street, how often do we remember that this person was once a child, usually one who was repeatedly traumatized, often a graduate of the foster care system?

THE ROLE OF THE FAMILY

As described in the previous section, the role of the family in the lives of people who become homeless is often toxic. During adolescence and young adulthood, many of these individuals lose a meaningful connection with their families. Subsequently, when they run into trouble in their lives, they can't rely on their families for safety. Other youth who come from healthier families and who develop psychiatric symptoms during their adolescence, presumably from obscure biological or genetic events, are often driven by their symptoms to leave their families. With no employable skills and preoccupied by their delusions or hallucinations, they drift onto the streets, while their parents, desperate to support them, are forced to watch helplessly. In some of the latter cases, families, lacking any meaningful support from the local government or service system, become worn out by the never-ending, unpredictable, dramatic, and frightening symptoms of their afflicted relatives and give up trying to help them. In either case, the impact of losing connection with their families cannot be overstated. The youth become isolated and adrift, forced to deal with the ravages of their illnesses without any source of emotional or tangible support. It is important to recognize that this downhill spiral is not inevitable. In many Western European countries whose governments provide more assistance to families, and where the family structure is tighter to begin with, mentally ill people often continue to live with their families, and homelessness is much less common.

THE VALUES OF AMERICAN SOCIETY

Though largely hidden and unrecognized, the values of American society have historically acted as powerful and pernicious forces in the etiology of homelessness. Mentally ill people who fail to live up to these values are often pushed to the margins of society and abandoned. Faced with even a small reversal of their finances or mental states and lacking any real source of economic or emotional support from their families or government, they have nowhere to go but the streets. Six values that affect the creation and perpetuation of homelessness are discussed below.

DEMOGRAPHIC HOMOGENEITY

First is the value our country places on demographic homogeneity. Although we celebrate the melting pot and diversity in theory, we are ambivalent in practice about the differences that exist among us. Differences are often negatively valued and deeply stigmatized. This can be seen in our intolerance of diversity based on race, religion, national origin, sexual orientation, and disabilities of all kinds. In the case of people who are homeless and mentally ill, with their profound poverty and strange behaviors, these differences blind us to the ways we are similar and make it difficult for us to identify with, connect to, and empathize with them. Our inability to see them first and foremost as human beings like the rest of us is the first step in a process of dehumanization, where we see them as devalued others. We regard them with blame, fear, hate, and disgust and punish them for their differentness by various acts of omission and commission, as though they had willingly brought their psychiatric symptoms and poverty on themselves or had been too careless and irresponsible to prevent these problems.

The fundamental attribution error, as coined by a Stanford psychology professor, describes how we blame others when bad things happen to them but blame external situations when bad things happen to us (Healy, 2017). This leads to the misconception that losing your home, for example, is due to who you are and the choices you have made rather than on the desperate circumstances of your life. We often think, "Why don't these people simply pull themselves together, get a job, and get off the streets?" This view in turn saps any willingness to share resources with them and in the political arena gets expressed in the small amount of support we give to help them, though our stinginess is usually dressed up and concealed behind a lot of hypocritical fanfare. In what becomes a vicious cycle, depriving severely mentally ill people of a decent life keeps them symptomatic and impoverished, reinforces the ways they appear different, and makes us feel even more distant and disconnected from them, more likely to blame and turn away from them, and less likely to vote for the funding they need to escape their symptomatic, impoverished, and empty existence. And so the cycle of stigma turns.

An important example of our intolerance of differences is the way we mistreat people of color, which expresses itself in their disproportionate numbers among the homeless. Although black people make up just 12 percent of the population, they account for 39 percent of the homeless population (HUD, 2021). As long as racism and its economic and social consequences continue to play such a ubiquitous role in American life, homelessness among this subpopulation is likely to continue.

SEGREGATION

The second value contributing to America's persistent homelessness is our inclination to segregate those we stigmatize as different. This practice has a long and cherished history in the United States—whether it was directed toward the separation of the races or expressed in the restriction of the Indigenous population to reservations, the isolation of Japanese people during the Second World War, or jailing or banishment of mentally ill people to the streets. The practice of segregating poor mentally ill people from the rest of society by keeping them on the streets is now accepted as a legitimate means of dealing with them, notwithstanding how much this aggravates their problems and entrenches them in their homeless state. The same practice has led to large numbers of mentally ill people (20 to 40 percent) in jails and prisons (Butterfield, 1999).

As described elsewhere, our impulse to segregate them is also expressed in the ubiquitous NIMBY movement that opposes the siting of shelters and low-cost supportive housing to anywhere but the poorest communities, where they largely live out of sight from those with greater means. Whatever the reasons we use to justify their segregation, such a practice further dehumanizes them and contributes to the large phenomenon of homelessness in the United States.

SELF-RELIANCE AND PRODUCTIVITY

The third value that creates and perpetuates homelessness is the importance American society places on self-reliance, independence, and productivity. People who, for whatever reason, don't have the capacity to meet their own needs and are forced to depend on others are often disparaged and devalued. The personal characteristic of self-reliance has perhaps become idealized because it played such an important role in the history of the United States. The process of colonization probably tended to self-select those who were endowed with this trait. It was also important for survival in a young country whose westward push into unknown territories had no structures available to provide help and protection. People were forced to live or die by their own wits, work, and talents. Having pulled themselves up by their own bootstraps, those who were successful came to believe that they deserved what they had made of themselves and that others who could not make it on their own, regardless of their personal, sometimes inborn, limitations or the social conditions in which they were raised, were deserving of nothing more than censure, contempt, and the impoverished life they were forced to lead. Helping such people, except in certain limited ways, is condemned as infantilizing them, which in turn would encourage their total dependency.

The result is that we've come to tolerate, accept, and justify the misery of people who can't make it on their own. Those who need society's support for their survival are treated as undeserving precisely because they need it. The paltry level of government benefits these people receive is the economic expression of the contempt in which we hold them. Even children cannot escape this hostile and withholding stance, as can be seen from the 15 million whom we allow to go hungry (Children's Defense Fund, 2020) and from the many casualties of the poorly funded and supervised foster care system in the United States. In the fight for survival, poor mentally ill people who can't meet the standard of self-sufficiency are left behind. The most vulnerable of them become homeless.

UNEQUAL OPPORTUNITY

The fourth value underlying our nation's homelessness is the way we debase the principle of equality of opportunity. While in theory we idealize the belief that all people should enjoy the equal opportunity to thrive in this society, we ignore and actively oppose it in practice. The fact is that this value has real meaning only if people either begin life from the same position on the starting line or are given help to compensate for handicaps that initially put them behind. The first condition, that people are equal from the start, is obviously a myth. And the second, that those who are disadvantaged from the outset will be given society's help to overcome their limitations, is honored only in dire circumstances. If we truly believed in the value of equal opportunity, we would create ways to level the playing field. In fact, we do the opposite. We have developed a school system that is partially dependent on local real estate taxes, which vary dramatically across different regions of any given state. The inequality in the local tax base is often reflected in a state's school systems. The poorest communities that need the best financed schools to help their kids rise out of poverty often get the worst as a result. In these cases, we have stacked the deck of opportunity against those at the bottom right from the get-go.

FREE-MARKET SOCIETY AND THE CONCENTRATION OF WEALTH

The fifth value is the one we place on our free-market society and the unbridled way it operates. Deeply entrenched in the economic structure of American society is the belief that people are entitled to keep and accumulate a very large share of what they earn or acquire, which has led to the vast concentration of wealth in the hands of a small minority of the population. A recent publication of the Federal Reserve has reported that the top 1 percent of US households holds fifteen times more wealth than the bottom 50 percent combined. Moreover, this wealth gap has steadily increased over the past three decades. The federal government estimates that the wealthiest 10 percent of Americans hold more than 88 percent of all equity in corporations and mutual fund shares, with just the top 1 percent of Americans controlling more than twice as much equity as the bottom 50 percent of Americans (Beer, 2020). Given the strong association between race and homelessness, it is important to note that the median net worth of black households was one-tenth that of white households. Black families are 40 percent less likely to own their own homes than white families (Hansen, 2020).

American billionaires have grown significantly richer during the COVID-19 pandemic. For example, Elon Musk crossed the $100 billion benchmark in August 2021 and saw his wealth increase by 242 percent over the first eight months of 2020. The top 10 percent of US households have seen their wealth rise by almost 10 percent while the total wealth controlled by the bottom 50 percent has been cut nearly in half (Beer, 2020).

Homeless mentally ill people are the most extreme and visible casualties of this vastly unequal distribution, although the causal connection between the two is largely ignored. While we have come to accept and justify this situation as the natural order of things, the fact is that there is nothing natural about it. It is the result of unfettered market forces and is supported by both our income and estate tax provisions. The first allows a small group of people to retain a huge and disproportionate share of the money they make. The second allows them to perpetuate their extreme economic advantage into future generations, guaranteeing that their descendants maintain this advantage through no efforts or talents of their own.

The shadow side of this system is that people who we've born into poverty through no fault of their own and who begin life behind the starting line have little chance of acquiring wealth during their lifetimes and have nothing but their poverty to pass onto their descendants, who in turn will begin life behind the next starting line. And so the cycle of poverty continues for generation after generation of poor people. Homeless mentally ill people are arguably trapped on the lowest rung of a steep economic ladder that has its feet virtually underground. When we pass them by, we conveniently ignore the obvious inequalities that they faced and instead blame them for their poverty and symptoms, allowing us to justify our refusal to help them. The real question is whether homelessness can ever be solved on a national scale by specific targeted programs, however well intentioned, unless we bring about more fundamental changes in the economic structure of society and the way wealth is distributed.

HOUSING AS A PRIVILEGE, NOT A RIGHT

The sixth value underlying our homelessness problem is the fact that housing is considered a privilege to be earned, not a human right granted to all citizens. The result is that having a home can be dispensed with or withheld at will—usually at the will of people who have homes and feel no sense of connection with people who have none. Underlying this is the belief that homelessness is a personal failure, not a social one. As such, it has been punished by governmental inattention, not ameliorated as a matter of right. Why should citizens contribute their hard-earned money to solving this problem when homeless people are themselves to blame for their plight? This conviction, though usually not stated explicitly, underlies public policy in our highly individualistic society that deplores dependency, prizes self-sufficiency, and casts blame on the unlucky.

Among frequent expressions about homeless people are "These people have obviously done something wrong," "Besides, they prefer life on the streets to having a home," "If they take drugs, what do they expect—our sympathy?" and "Why don't they get a job?" The conclusion that follows these refrains is that homeless people haven't earned the privilege of having a home and that until they do, "They're lucky we give them anything." Because this is society's dominant view, solving the problem of homelessness has received short shrift.

It is worth noting that in contrast to the United States, the United Nations has long embraced housing as a human right in Article 25 of the UN's Universal Declaration of Human Rights, adopted in 1948 and signed by 130 nations. The executive branch of the US government became a signatory to the declaration but failed to persuade the Senate to ratify its signature, making it impossible to bring the article to life. European Union countries have also affirmed this principle in their Charter for Fundamental Rights, which states that "In order to combat social exclusion and poverty, the Union recognizes and respects the right to social and housing assistance to ensure a decent existence for all those who lack sufficient resources" (Official Journal at the European Communities, 2000). Even in Europe, however, the right to housing was eroded after the recession of 2008, when European cities experienced increases in homelessness, demonstrating that even rights are not exempt from large social and economic forces. They can be taken away, as well as given, and constant vigilance and political action is necessary to protect them. Enshrining housing as a human right may be a precondition for a fairer struggle of poor people in the marketplace but is in no way a panacea or guarantee.

THE SELF-PERPETUATING
NATURE OF HOMELESSNESS

Once people with mental illness become homeless, it is very difficult for them to escape it. This is largely due to the drastic effects of homelessness on every aspect of their lives. In addition to compromising their physical health and fragile psychological stability, living on the street aggravates their symptoms, wears down their bodies, increases their illegal drug use, and increases their vulnerability to criminalization. The chaos of their lives makes it difficult for them to keep appointments, access services, and find and maintain employment. Homelessness also makes it impossible for them to carry, store, and take their psychiatric medications, even if they are willing to do so. Medication is often lost, stolen, traded for illegal drugs, or simply forgotten in the chaos of street life. With each passing year, their symptoms become worse and their physical and emotional state deteriorate. Homelessness saps their energy and kills any vision they might have had for their futures. Life is filled with danger, physical privation, boredom, depression, and despair. Whatever shred of self-esteem they might have had before becoming homeless is usually lost in the face of the humiliation, hatred, and blame they experience every day from those who pass them on the street. They are viewed as dirt and come to identify themselves as such. Their only respite from the street occurs in hospitals and jails, but after leaving these institutions, they almost inevitably end up back on the streets. These and other consequences of homelessness make it difficult for mentally ill people to "pull themselves together" and find a way out of their grim existence. Life on the street becomes a self-perpetuating condition. And death comes early, on average, at fifty years of age.

As mentally ill people try to escape the streets, they find themselves confronting not just one governmental mistake or misguided public policy but the combined effects of the way they are stigmatized, the prejudices of the culture, and the injurious policies and budgets of multiple governmental systems (health care, mental health, social welfare, employment, public housing, public works, criminal justice, and the courts). The casualties we see on the street reflect a social consensus that poor people with mental illness are less human than the rest of us, that the current conditions of homeless mentally ill people in America are tolerable, and that these people don't deserve more than they're getting.

SUMMARY OF CAUSES OF HOMELESSNESS

Many factors have led to the crisis of homelessness. Among them are the following:

- *Deinstitutionalization*—Deinstitutionalization was poorly conceptualized and implemented by state governments, which led to the discharge of hundreds of thousands of patients from state mental hospitals and made it difficult for patients to gain admission or readmission to these facilities. The mentally ill had few allies that could have helped shape this process in a way that was more humane.
- *Side effects of psychiatric medication*—Many mentally ill people are reluctant to take psychiatric medications in part because of the disturbing side effects of these drugs. Untreated psychoses and perpetuation of homelessness are the results.
- *Drug epidemic*—The epidemic of street drugs has infected broad swaths of poor neighborhoods in the United States.

This has led to dependence on these substances, which, while providing some temporary relief, has contributed to the aggravation of people's psychiatric symptoms and is one of the major causes of homelessness.

- *Holes in the federal and state safety net*—The safety net programs created by federal and state governments (SSI, Medicaid, Medicare, and supportive housing) have historically been so poorly funded that many poor mentally ill people who depend on them can barely survive, are pushed onto the streets, and can't pull themselves out once they land there. The gaps in these programs are largely a result of the stigma carried by these people and their resultant lack of political and economic power. They simply can't effectively advocate for themselves when government resources are allocated.

- *Inadequate community mental health programs*—Community mental health programs were impoverished and poorly conceptualized from the outset of deinstitutionalization, leaving mentally ill patients without adequate case management support.

- *Psychiatric treatment in general hospitals*—Economic incentives led to closures of hospitals and a dwindling supply of psychiatric beds. State and federal governments and insurance companies were all culprits in promoting this phenomenon. A lack of beds in turn results in obstacles to the admission of very sick patients, premature discharges, and the use of the streets as an "acceptable" discharge option. The revolving door in and out of hospitals has become commonplace in many cities.

- *Restrictive interpretation of commitment laws*—Adding to the above restrictions on general hospital treatment is the courts' practice of prematurely discharging many people to the street who have a very limited ability to care for themselves. The problem is the very restrictive criteria used by the courts in defining "grave disability," even when many of the mentally ill people they evaluate can barely find anything to eat, have no place to sleep, and are in extreme physical danger on the streets. Many people end up homeless or in jail. It is almost as if the courts, in interpreting involuntary commitment legislation, have accommodated to the inadequate supply of psychiatric hospital beds.

- *Criminalization of the mentally ill*—The use of state hospitals to confine and segregate the mentally ill has been replaced by jails, often for minor nuisance crimes. After their release, these people are dumped back onto the street with no money, no treatment, and no housing. Recidivism is high as a result.

- *Lack of affordable housing*—A lack of permanent, affordable housing with clinical support is the most important cause of homelessness. This results from gentrification of existing low-cost housing; cutbacks in federal support for low-cost housing; a shift in the balance between supply and demand for such housing; restrictive zoning requirements, which impede the creation of new affordable housing; the failure of cities to establish set-asides for homeless mentally ill people; insufficient protections for people at risk of homelessness; and the unwillingness of many city governments to challenge the NIMBY opposition to new housing for mentally ill people.

- *Problems of shelters*—Many mentally ill people find the so-called shelter system, with its insufficient number of beds, to be dangerous, humiliating, and unacceptable as an alternative to the street.

- *Adverse childhood events and the poorly funded foster care system*—The relatively large number of people who experienced serious and pervasive adverse events in their childhoods and the glaring inadequacies of the social service, foster care, and juvenile justice systems are a major cause of homelessness. As much as 50 percent of the adult homeless mentally ill population experienced foster care early in their lives.
- *Inadequate government support for families of mentally ill people*—Families experience great difficulty in caring for their mentally ill relatives, whose constant crises and complicated symptoms often lead to ruptured relationships and lost financial and emotional support.
- *The values of American society*—These American values include our ambivalence about differentness, our use of segregation on the streets and in jails to isolate and marginalize others, our idealization of self-reliance and productivity, our acceptance of unequal opportunity at the starting line of peoples' lives, our acceptance of great disparities of wealth, and our view of housing as a privilege, not a right.
- *The self-perpetuating nature of homelessness*—The self-perpetuating nature makes it almost impossible for people who are poor and mentally ill to escape the streets once they have become homeless.
- *The crushing burden of stigma*—Poor mentally ill people are forced to bear crushing stigma, a burden that becomes more severe when they become homeless. We are much more attuned to the ways we are different from them than the ways we are the same. We lose the capacity to identify or empathize with them when all we see are their rags, carts, and strange behaviors. The way we devalue and dehumanize them is the most fundamental and underlying cause of homelessness for it leads to many other more proximate causes.

SOLUTIONS

Given the powerful social, cultural, and economic forces that contribute to homelessness among the mentally ill, we have to ask whether this problem can possibly be solved if these forces are left unchanged. Perhaps their existence explains why the gap between what we know can help these people and what we actually do to help them is so enormous. How much progress can we make if adverse childhood events remain so prevalent and their effects left unaddressed, if disparities in wealth are accepted as natural and God-given, if the effects of racism in this country remain so tenacious, if American values remain so firmly rooted in individualism and self-reliance, if cities become wealthy at the expense of their poorest citizens, if the drug epidemic continues to ravage our streets, if the family structure in America remains so strained and fragile for many people, if criminalization of mental illness and homelessness is the go-to solution for people whose primary crime is being different and disadvantaged, if the so-called social safety net remains so filled with holes, if people who are desperately poor and mentally ill continue to be so profoundly stigmatized and held responsible for their plight, if a large minority of well-connected citizens can't find it within themselves to be generous to their less fortunate brethren and continue to actively oppose the siting of affordable housing in their communities, if housing remains unaffordable to so many people and is viewed as a privilege that must be earned and not a human right?

If these forces remain so stubbornly entrenched and continue to exert such a powerful influence, we may exhaust ourselves attempting to solve the problem and have nothing much to show for it but a patchwork of incomplete, often short-lived, narrowly targeted programs, each of which addresses only a small piece of the problem.

And yet the nihilistic conclusion of doing nothing while we wait for these forces to magically disappear seems totally unacceptable and irresponsible. Nor would this be reasonable, from a human or economic standpoint. Moreover, examples of successes exist in various parts of the country with different population groups. These examples are important because of what they can teach us, serving as a catalyst for inspiration and a compass for action. They are also meaningful because they can challenge the prevailing pessimism that exists in dealing with this problem. In fact, pessimism itself has been an obstacle to progress for it has led to the self-fulfilling prophecy where people fail to act because they believe it is fruitless.

In contemplating the obstacles to progress, it is important to remember that the social and economic forces responsible for the oppression of other groups, however intractable and immutable they once seemed, ultimately yielded to the unrelenting pressure of people who were determined to face them down. In fact, the sudden and seemingly unpredictable shift in these forces ultimately led to the acceptance of women's suffrage, the New Deal, the civil rights movement, gay marriage, the Me Too movement, and Black Lives Matter. Each of these revolutions seemed impossible before it happened. As Martin Luther King Jr. once famously said, "The arc of the moral universe is long, but it bends toward justice" (King,

1958). And as Margaret Mead argued, "Never doubt that a small group of thoughtful, committed citizens can change the world. Indeed, it's the only thing that ever has" (Lutkehaus, 2008). Progress often takes years of struggle in which nothing seems to change until some invisible tipping point is reached, when the forces of resistance suddenly collapse and radical change unexpectedly occurs. This is how we must regard the battle against homelessness. It will take longer than any of us wish, but it will happen.

EXAMPLES OF SUCCESS

In contrast to San Francisco with its meager 1,200 shelter beds for over 5,000 unsheltered homeless people, New York City created a large number of shelter beds as a result of the lawsuit *Callahan v. Carey* (1979), which relied on a "right to shelter" clause in the New York State Constitution. This led to a consent decree that required the city to provide as many shelter beds as were needed by people who would otherwise be forced to sleep on the streets. The city also penalizes people who refuse to use the shelter system. It thus uses both a carrot and stick approach. The result is that New York City now has 68,000 shelter beds, leaving relatively few people unsheltered each night and serving as compelling evidence that when cities are forced to do so, they are able to find solutions to most of the obstacles they complain are insuperable. The rate of unsheltered homelessness in New York City is now 45 per 100,000 residents versus San Francisco's 492 per 100,000, less than one-tenth on a per-population basis compared to San Francisco. I emphasize the experience of New

York City because it provides proof that the problem is solvable if enough political will can be generated to do so, whether by the courts or by popular demand. If New York City, with all its complexities and challenges, is able to provide shelter for over 60,000 very compromised people, other cities can also.

Unfortunately, the right to permanent housing, as opposed to temporary shelter, was not included in the New York State Constitution, and a dearth of such housing is the result. People are stuck in shelters for years waiting for permanent housing. The average length of stay in a shelter is 414 days for a single adult, 580 days for an adult family, and 446 days for a family with children—the highest it's been in each category in the last five years (DiPrinzio, 2019). If New York City had been forced to create permanent housing units in the same way it was forced to create shelter beds, the city would likely have been able to do so. Similarly, it is highly likely that San Francisco, were it compelled to do so, would find ways of creating shelter beds for its unsheltered population, notwithstanding all the political hand-wringing about the impossible obstacles that block its efforts. In most of the country, and in the absence of judicial action, cities are free to choose between creating shelter beds and permanent housing and too often do neither robustly.

Additional evidence that the problem of homelessness can be solved is the 46 percent drop in the rate of homelessness among veterans between 2010 and 2019. In this case, progress was due to the publicity and ensuing political storm surrounding the nation's abandonment of these people once they returned from serving their country in the Middle East. Moreover, this success occurred throughout the United States despite local variations in the state of housing in individual cities, demonstrating that whatever the unique obstacles were in each city, the pressure to overcome them ultimately triumphed.

When solutions to the lack of housing for mentally ill homeless people are proposed, cities often claim that they are impractical and can't be implemented for various reasons, such as cost, neighborhood opposition, and lack of availability. It is thus instructive to examine the response of San Francisco to the need for such beds when COVID-19 struck. After the city discovered that 57 percent of one shelter's residents had contracted COVID, it moved aggressively to reduce the number of beds in each shelter and create additional shelter beds elsewhere, quickly pushing through obstacles it previously argued were insuperable. Fearing a public health catastrophe among the homeless that might spread to the general population, the city established shelter beds in tent complexes, gyms, convention centers, and empty hotel rooms. While these initiatives deserve applause, they also demonstrate that solutions were always available but unrealized until the risk of a greater political crisis than homelessness itself shook the city government out of its torpor. Why did it take this kind of emergency to prod San Francisco and other cities facing the same problem into action in finding or creating beds that thousands of unsheltered people have needed for decades?

The federal government's dramatic response to the COVID pandemic raises the same question. After arguing for years that it didn't have the funds to help solve the homeless crisis for people with and without mental illness, it suddenly discovered billions of dollars to buy vaccines for the general population. When the general population stands to benefit, not just homeless mentally ill people, solutions that were always at hand but not enacted seem to magically appear from nowhere. It seems only fair to ask whether we can believe politicians in the future when they declare that no solutions to homelessness can be found. Just as in the case of New York City that took action only when forced to do so (i.e., by the court), other cities found solutions that they had previously declared were impossible—but only when the politics of the pandemic demanded such action.

As mentioned in the previous chapter, the citizens of San Francisco, in 2018, approved ballot measure Proposition C, which will generate $300 million to provide housing and shelters for homeless people through a surtax on certain very wealthy companies. There is no reason that such a ballot initiative can't be replicated in other cities. What San Francisco lacked, unfortunately, was a specific provision that a certain portion of the housing that will be created must be used for homeless mentally ill people. It remains to be seen whether the mentally ill will have a place, other than last in line, when the funds are allocated.

In 2022, the California state government enacted legislation that requires cities to draw up plans for the creation of low-income housing and would allow the state to override local zoning restrictions if these threatened to defeat such housing. This was an important victory for low-income people in the state and if implemented wisely, with units set aside for homeless mentally ill people, would help eliminate a major obstacle to the creation of housing for these people. This legislation should be replicated in other states.

The foregoing successes after years of inaction imply that our failures to provide housing for homeless people more generally, and for homeless mentally ill people specifically, have not resulted from a lack of knowledge or a lack of successful examples of how to do it but from a lack of the will to implement what we know. Obstacles that appear insurmountable for financial, political, or operational reasons get swept aside when governments develop the will and become serious about overcoming them. The "We can't do this because . . ." response to hurdles simply can't be allowed to perpetuate homelessness in one city after another. When the political forces that demand a solution to the lack of affordable housing for mentally ill people are greater than the forces that create and maintain the problem, we will solve it. Proposition C, enacted in San Francisco, provides evidence that when the citizens of a city get frustrated with politicians' lackluster efforts to make a real dent in the problem of homelessness, they can take action and do something about it.

Before enumerating solutions for the people who are already homeless, it is crucial to emphasize the importance of preventing new people from becoming homeless. Most of the articles in the press, as well as our immediate visceral experience in seeing homeless people as we walk through our cities, lead us to focus on people who are already living on the street and ignore the factors that will inevitably create the next generation of homeless people. But unless we stem the flow of new people onto the streets, we will fail to reduce the overall numbers of homeless people. Those we manage with tremendous effort to remove will simply be replaced by people who are newly homeless. This has happened over the last several years and partially accounts for why we have failed to move the needle and have seen an increase, not a decrease, in the prevalence of homelessness in the United States. In San Francisco alone, for every one person who is housed, an estimated three more are becoming homeless. Since many of the solutions to help people who are already homeless overlap with those necessary to prevent new additions to the streets, I have chosen to identify and not separate them. Rather, I have divided this section on specific solutions into those that address the problems of housing, services (including tracking, job and housing support, linkage, and services for high-risk youths), and the legal system.

HOUSING

This section on solutions begins with a focus on housing since this is the most crucial intervention for both prevention and helping those already homeless. It includes interventions that create low-cost, affordable housing and shelters; supportive housing for those who need it; and the use of a housing-first policy. It seems obvious that the basic solution to homelessness is to provide people with homes. People who are mentally ill additionally need case management services, but without a home little mental health intervention can be done. Providing housing is thus the central action around which all else must revolve, whether we are attempting to prevent homelessness for youth who age out of the foster care system or helping a person who is already unsheltered on the street escape from his or her homeless state. Almost every other solution to the problem of homelessness discussed below depends on the availability of adequate low-cost housing. Without it, almost none of these other solutions will work.

PROVIDE AFFORDABLE HOUSING FOR MENTALLY ILL HOMELESS OR THOSE AT RISK FOR HOMELESSNESS

The precondition for the success of each of these suggestions is not the availability of know-how as much as it is the availability of political will that cities must develop to implement them. What does this mean in practical terms? Strategies must be multipronged: they must protect renters who are unstably housed and increase the overall supply of affordable new housing.

- Stabilize people who are tenuously housed. This involves, among other things, establishing rent controls so that people don't lose their housing because their existing apartments suddenly become unaffordable. While landlords inevitably object to these measures, without them, the kind of wealth-driven increases in rents that have accounted for so much of the nation's homelessness will continue to occur.
- Institute procedures to protect people from no-fault evictions, establish an appeals mechanism for people who are threatened with such evictions, and give these renters sufficient compensation to find other housing.

- Require landlords to rent a portion of their vacant units to homeless mentally ill people or those about to become homeless. Establishing a vacancy tax or paying landlords above-market rents to lease to homeless people are examples of incentivizing landlords to set aside some of their units for this purpose. In San Francisco, for example, 33,000 units were vacant in 2020 for various reasons. In Vancouver, British Columbia, the vacancy rate is 2.6 percent (Daily Hive Vancouver Staff, 2021). In many cities, Airbnb rentals have taken thousands of units off the long-term rental market. An ordinance recently enacted in San Francisco dramatically reduced the number of Airbnb units in the city, essentially increasing the available housing stock. While not all vacant units can be converted to housing for homeless people, many could be. Moreover, this type of intervention is much more efficient, economical, and faster than most other solutions to the lack of housing.

- Provide short-term financial assistance to people who suddenly find themselves at imminent risk of losing their housing. This method has been proven to prevent homelessness. In 2009, the federal government under President Barack Obama established the Homelessness Prevention and Rapid Re-Housing Program, which did just this. In the first two years of the program, 900,000 people were prevented from becoming homeless and 250,000 who had already lost their housing were rapidly rehoused, thus sparing them the fate of becoming chronically homeless. Of the latter group, 89 percent were permanently housed at the time they exited the program (HUD, 2016). Like so many programs, this one lost its funding, but not before it had demonstrated that homelessness could be dramatically reduced if sufficient political will could be mobilized and directed to the challenge.

- Expand the affordable housing stock and create set-asides for homeless mentally ill people. Among the interventions that would accomplish this are, first, the enactment of regulations restricting the wholesale conversion and elimination of the affordable housing that already exists. The experience of many cities has been that in the absence of laws regulating gentrification, conversion of low-cost housing to condominiums that are then sold to people with higher incomes has diminished the amount of affordable housing. Second, laws and regulations need to be enacted that loosen zoning laws and ease restrictions on the construction of new affordable housing. Unless these and other steps are taken, the affordable housing stock in the United States will continue to decline and ultimately defeat attempts to solve the problem of homelessness. Every person who newly gains access to housing will simply displace another person who loses it, resulting in a net gain of zero. This cruel form of musical chairs is one of the major reasons that programs offering housing assistance to homeless people but don't increase the total supply of affordable housing have failed to decrease the number of homeless people in many cities. The conclusion seems obvious that the federal government, with its disproportionately large tax base, must step in to help cities and states increase their low-income housing stock and that, in exchange for government support, developers be required to set aside a significant portion of their units for homeless mentally ill people or those about to become homeless. While there are currently requirements in certain cities for low-cost housing set-asides, these are generally not targeted for people who are homeless or about to become so. It cannot be emphasized enough that simply expanding the amount of so-called affordable, low-cost housing will not solve the problem of homelessness unless critical set-asides are required for homeless people, including those for homeless mentally ill people.

- Place a surcharge on the taxes of large, wealthy companies that disproportionately benefit from cities' infrastructures and employment pools, and use these funds to create and fund housing for homeless people, as San Francisco recently did.
- Undertake class-action litigation to hold cities and states responsible for creating shelters and low-cost housing for homeless mentally ill people.
- Stand up to the efforts of citizens who attempt to prevent the creation of affordable housing in their communities. Unless NIMBY is replaced by YIMBY (yes in my backyard), people who are suffering the effects of homelessness, mental illness, and stigma will continue to be forced to live on the streets. Too often politicians stay silent when they should publicly oppose this kind of destructive activism.

Opponents of government efforts to mitigate some of the negative behaviors of the marketplace often claim that government has no business enacting rent-control legislation, opposing no-fault evictions, or placing a surcharge on the tax of wealthy companies, whose highly paid employees drive up the demand for housing and increase its cost. These matters are essentially private, not public, they argue. But, as indicated earlier, without such interference, unrestrained market forces and their negative consequences will continue to wreak havoc on the lives of very poor people and act as feeder systems for homelessness. Economic prosperity for some will paradoxically continue to create financial pain for others.

Opponents of such "interference" might do well to remember the advantages government gives to people wealthy enough to own their homes, which are far out of reach for people who are very poor and at risk of homelessness. Specifically, they might take note of the fact that government "meddling" in the private marketplace is exactly what allows them to deduct their mortgage interest payments when they prepare their taxes, a tax advantage that, in aggregate, amounts to a $140 billion hit to the federal budget (McCarty et al., 2019). Government "interference" is also responsible for the favorable treatment of certain institutions that provide funding for home loans or facilitate a secondary market for home mortgages (e.g., Federal Home Loan Banks, Fannie Mae, Freddie Mac, and Ginnie Mae). It has also led to federal programs that insure lenders against losses on home loans (e.g., the VA and USDA mortgage-guarantee programs), provide funding to organizations that counsel prospective homebuyers on obtaining homeownership, and grant monies that can be used to provide down-payment and closing-cost assistance to eligible homebuyers. The faction opposing government "interference" for poor people might do well to remember all these examples of welfare for the middle class when they decry the comparatively small amount of government help to the poor. Is government interference legitimate only when people of means are the ones who benefit?

Placing homeless mentally ill people in housing often requires that this be accompanied by either off-site case managers (i.e., individual clinicians) or clinicians who are part of assertive community treatment (ACT) teams or that are located in apartment houses (i.e., supported housing). Permanent supportive housing provides wrap-around on-site services for tenants to help them organize their lives, assist them in getting treatment for their addictions and psychiatric problems, provide them crisis intervention services when they start to come unglued, link them to sources of government support, and help them find supported vocational or day treatment programs so they have something to do all day other than walk around the streets or languish in their rooms. As indicated above, although it is usually assumed that creating supportive housing is prohibitively expensive, many studies have demonstrated that homelessness itself is even more expensive. Despite the skepticism that initially greeted the supportive housing model, the data show that 70 to 80 percent of homeless people who are placed in such housing remain stably housed one year after their placements. Also, research in Chicago showed that because this model led to an improvement in their functional status, it resulted in a 29 percent reduction in hospital stays and a 24 percent reduction in emergency department visits (Sadowski et al., 2009). Further evidence can be seen from the successful use of this approach for homeless veterans, which I cited earlier. This and other evidence demonstrate that if the right kind of housing is created, people will effectively use it if offered. It also debunks the myth that people are homeless because they're beyond help or want to live on the street.

UTILIZE A HOUSING-FIRST POLICY IN DETERMINING ACCESS TO HOUSING

Beyond these fundamental solutions to the housing problem, the regulations governing access to housing need to be reformed, and the organizational design of such housing needs to be modernized in accordance with the plethora of evidence available. Housing needs to be provided as the first intervention, without preconditions, before requiring that people become clean and sober or take psychiatric medications as entrance criteria. This has been called the housing-first approach to homelessness. It is the complete antithesis of the access criteria that have existed historically, which gave housing, however limited the supply, to people only after they stopped using drugs or complied with psychiatric treatment. Years of experience have proven that people generally can't stop using alcohol and drugs and can't possibly comply with psychiatric treatment unless and until they are safely housed. The problems, stresses, and seductions of the street are just too intense. One of the people I interviewed told me, "You've got to either be stoned or crazy to survive the streets. There's no other way." The old approach essentially placed housing out of reach for some of the very people who needed it most.

INCREASE THE NUMBER, QUALITY, AND TYPE OF SHELTERS

While there is no substitute for permanent supportive housing, cities should create temporary shelters while the latter is developed. Allowing people to sleep completely unsheltered, at the mercy of the elements, during the very long period it takes to create something more permanent is cruel. Cities have taken different approaches to this problem, as demonstrated by the contrast between New York City and San Francisco described above. Moreover, when cities do create shelters, they need to design these very differently than they have done before. Shelters need to do more than just put a roof over people's heads. They also need to engage difficult clients, provide them clinical and logistical support, and link them to housing when this becomes available.

Over the last few years in San Francisco, a new form of shelter, called a Navigation Center, has been developed. It differs from traditional shelters in that people can move in with their partners, pets, and belongings and can remain until they find permanent housing instead of having to stand in line night after night while they hope for a bed and, assuming they are offered one, to be kicked out early the next morning. These shelters also have clinicians that provide people intensive counseling and case management and help them navigate the difficult housing market, a function from which the shelter takes its name. These centers are twice as expensive as traditional shelters and are in very short supply, but they've proven successful at finding permanent housing for more than half of the 3,000 people who have used them in the last three years. Whether these centers will make a dent in the homeless problem in San Francisco remains to be seen and is likely to depend on how many the city creates, as well as what other steps it takes to mitigate the economic forces that have transformed San Francisco into a homeless epicenter of the nation.

SERVICES

The solutions I described above are primarily focused on how to address the lack of housing for people who are homeless and mentally ill. But these solutions need to be understood in a broader framework. However crucial an individual's need for housing is and however important it is to solve their biological need for shelter, it fails to address many of their other needs. Just as their diagnosis and psychiatric symptoms do not define them, neither does their need for housing. Having a roof over one's head, imperative as it is, does not constitute a life. A home is a prerequisite for the fulfillment of many important needs, but without deliberate attention to them, they will remain unmet.

BEYOND HOUSING

Because the obstacles to solving the primary need for housing are so challenging, it may seem naïve and idealistic to remind ourselves of the fact that mentally ill people, like the rest of us, have other needs as well—the need for autonomy, the need for participation and inclusion in society, the need to be accorded the rights and privileges of citizenship enjoyed by the rest of us, the need to live with purpose, and the need for friendship. Unfortunately, the fight for basic services and subsistence has been so difficult that a fundamental rationale for deinstitutionalization, inclusion of people with mental illness into society, has often been lost in the bare struggle for survival.

Living in society is very different from being included in it—the first being a geographic fact, the second a social and political one. Removing barriers to inclusion is not just a requirement of the service system; it is an obligation of society. Unless society is willing to actively involve people with mental illness in all spheres of social, political, and economic life, these individuals will continue to be deprived of one of their most important human rights. Participation in the workforce and inclusion in housing, neighborhoods, recreational activities, and religious institutions will require more than adequate mental health services. People with severe and chronic mental illness, now isolated on the streets or in apartments, will be shortchanged unless affirmative steps are taken to pull them back from the margins of society where they currently exist. Actions must be taken to counter the constant social undertow that leads to their isolation, whether this occurs in mental hospitals, in jails, or on the streets.

These measures can't wait until people's symptoms are treated. Treatment cannot occur first and inclusion second. A broken leg will heal with or without social relationships or inclusion in society. A broken mind will not. In fact, treatment for many people can be accomplished only in the context of inclusion. For this to occur, the community itself, not just the mentally ill individual, or the service system needs to change. Even if these needs are not as visible or dramatic as the need for a home, we will, if we ignore them, limit our aspirations, narrow the solutions we craft, and implement them mechanistically. People will be cloistered in their apartments, living with no meaning, aspirations, or vision for their future. They will have no vocational skills, no leisure time activities, no friendships, no interests, no opportunity to participate in community events. They may live in the community but will not be part of it, in which case the deadening, isolated, marginalized lives that mentally ill people led originally in mental hospitals, then on the streets, will simply be reproduced in their apartments. They will continue to view themselves as unwanted outcasts in a society that stigmatizes them. They may have achieved a roof over their heads but not much else. In summary, as we try to solve the problem of their homelessness, it is important to complement this with interventions that address their other human needs as well.

THE NEED FOR A TRACKING SYSTEM TO IDENTIFY HOMELESS MENTALLY ILL PEOPLE AND THEIR NEEDS

It seems obvious that a tracking system should be developed by cities so that they know who is homeless, who is about to become homeless, and what services each person by name requires. Without this, the system of care will act in a chaotic, inefficient manner; people will slip between the cracks and will not get what they need except by accident. While this suggestion seems trivial and bureaucratic, it is remarkable just how disorganized even well-meaning efforts can become when this information is not available. Of course, without more fundamental solutions, this one will simply catalog how bad things are and how much needs to be done for the people who are evaluated and tracked. Nevertheless, even this information would be useful in delineating the scope of the problem in each city and providing a framework for solving it.

It goes without saying that mentally ill people on the street need treatment, not just housing. The bedrock of an effective community mental health system is case management, whether the clinicians who fill the role work individually or in ACT teams. Case managers are critical people in the lives of the homeless. Never was a profession so perfectly misnamed since clients are not cases and they do not need to be managed. Case managers fulfill crucial functions in the lives of their clients—as clinicians, advocates, teachers, friends, guides, parental surrogates, and bridges between clients and services. Nothing is too big, too small, too dirty, or too mundane for the tasks these clinicians are asked to fulfill. Case managers provide or arrange what their clients need to live as full a life as they are capable.

The job is undeniably hard—one for smart, clinically trained, wise, patient, well-balanced people who can empathize with those who often don't want empathy, can tolerate frustration and disappointment, are not afraid to get involved in the nitty-gritty of their clients' lives, and can commit their hearts and brains to the work. They often have to scour the streets and bars in search of their clients, dealing with them as they are and where they are.

Case managers must engage clients who often want nothing to do with them and who have been taught through their experiences as children and adults and the failures of the service system not to trust anyone. These clients are certain they will be eventually deserted or disappointed by anyone who initially offers help. Moreover, they have become experts at making it likely that such predictions will be realized, so good are they at defeating and thwarting the attempts of the clinicians who are trying to help them. Sometimes they don't get what they need because they lack the basic skills to accept case managers' help, and sometimes their psychiatric and drug-related symptoms make it impossible for them to connect with case managers, no matter how caring and sophisticated the latter are.

Assuming that, over time, case managers can make human contact with their clients, through persistence, cajoling, or proving that they can help them get what they need (e.g., SSI, housing, medication, drug treatment, dental services), there is a chance that clients will begin to trust them. Without this kind of real human relationship, very little else is possible. Only if this connection is established can case managers teach their clients the skills that they either never developed or lost with the onset of their illness: how to shop; cook; do laundry; take care of an apartment; manage medications; budget money; use transportation; go to the movies, church, or synagogue; and keep themselves safe. And through this focus on their clients' concrete needs, case managers help them develop other skills relating to trust, attachment, and social relationships, as well as encouraging them to take psychiatric medications and resist their craving for drugs or other self-defeating behaviors. Case managers can also help them bridge the yawning gap between a solitary life and inclusion in society, sometimes acting as go-betweens, advocates, and negotiators to help them access society's mainstream institutions and activities.

As a result of all these functions, case managers are critical in preventing people from slipping into homelessness. By helping people manage the concrete aspects of their lives, money, housing, health, medications, or drug addictions, they help to stabilize people who are very fragile and often one step away from losing their housing and becoming homeless. Case managers also recognize and jump in when people are in crisis, when they are becoming more symptomatic, or when they are in danger of losing their housing and can help them regain their footing.

Many people remain homeless simply because they can't master the complicated application process for government benefits. Filling out onerous paperwork, interviewing, retrieving past records, and obtaining the statement of a psychiatrist are all required from people who often lack the resources to understand, much less satisfy, these requirements. How are such people possibly going to navigate this complicated multistep process? A simple intervention that many cities already use, but which needs to be expanded, is the act of deploying case managers to help people in the application processes. Doing so is also clearly in the financial interest of cities, who can then transfer some of their treatment and housing costs to the federal government.

There are two critical caveats. For case managers to be able to do their job effectively, their caseloads must be realistic. Too often, excellent and dedicated clinicians burn out simply because the system for which they work fails to recognize this. The most dedicated people are ultimately frustrated by being rendered ineffective, which inevitably leads to constant turnover in staff. Clients will then be faced with having to learn to trust another stranger. After repeated experiences of losing one clinician after another, clients will lose their faith and trust in the system. It is also crucial that clients not lose their case managers because the system is structured to push clients who have made progress to a lower intensity of treatment with new clinicians. Not only does this discourage the development of trust with their new case managers, whom clients know they will lose in this never-ending shuffle, but over time they tend to regress and lose their progress in the absence of the high-intensity service that helped them to advance in the first place.

In summary, without excellent case managers, a mental health system will tend to be mechanistic, impersonal, inaccessible, and exclusively focused on the management of symptoms. The core of clients' problems and human needs will be left untouched. After years of failure, the original promise of community mental health advanced by some clinicians, inclusion, participation, and integration into society will be a distant memory. A service system deficient in many respects can be partially rescued by an excellent case management program. But without the latter, there is little that a system can do to compensate.

Numerous demonstration projects have shown that individual case management or ACT teams can stabilize homeless people in the community and can either prevent or rescue mentally ill people from homelessness. The problem is that despite the fact that Medicaid now reimburses such interventions, states with caps on their Medicaid budgets severely restrict the generalization of these successful programs—yet another example that the problem is not a lack of knowledge of what works but our failure to implement what we know. The federal government has to pay a greater share of states' Medicaid budgets in order to solve this problem. The case management system is too important to be left to the budgetary restrictions of the states.

INCREASE THE AVAILABILITY AND ACCEPTABILITY OF SUBSTANCE ABUSE TREATMENT

Because of the high incidence of substance abuse among homeless people, it is imperative that cities take steps to make treatment more acceptable to them. Currently many people refuse to seek treatment because of rigid entrance requirements for sobriety that they initially can't meet. Lowering these barriers, utilizing a harm-reduction approach, reaching out to them on the street, and providing housing for them despite their drug use as a way to encourage their acceptance of treatment are all critical interventions if these people have any hope of getting into treatment. The same suggestions are relevant for people who are not homeless but are one step away from it because of the impact of drug abuse on their mental and financial state. Once they are driven to the streets by their drug use, it is more difficult to help them because the conditions of homelessness are so grim that they need drugs to endure it.

DEVELOP OPPORTUNITIES FOR VOCATIONAL TRAINING AND SUPPORTIVE EMPLOYMENT

Job training and supported employment are typically ignored when services are developed and funded. Work is so important in maintaining one's self-esteem, giving structure to one's life and time, stabilizing symptoms, and supporting one's adaptive and executive functions, among many other things, that without it, people will be excluded from a crucial aspect of life. They will also be disregarded and demeaned as lazy, feel useless, and remain as outsiders in a culture that prizes work as central and defining. Yet getting businesses to provide supported employment opportunities and governments to fund vocational assistance to mentally disabled people, with some exceptions, has been almost impossible. Unless governments actually accept responsibility for vocational services and incentivize businesses to pitch in—with some form of tax credit, for example—it is unlikely that this gap will ever be filled.

INCREASE THE AVAILABILITY OF PSYCHIATRIC BEDS IN GENERAL HOSPITALS

Many people with severe psychiatric symptoms end up on the streets because they have either been denied admission to general hospitals or discharged prematurely. It is crucial to address the causes of this practice. They include the lack of sufficient acute-care beds, the restrictive way that judges interpret state commitment laws, and the unrealistically high standard that Medicaid sets for defining medical necessity and reimbursing hospital care. At a minimum, the policy of eliminating hospital beds, despite the need for them, should be stopped and reversed. Judges should revise their interpretation of commitment laws, and the federal government should change the way it restricts payment to hospitals. While acute-care hospitals are not a permanent solution to the problem of homelessness, the need for these beds for highly symptomatic people is overwhelming in many cities, largely because of the unavailability of less medicalized settings.

The reform of Medicaid, by increasing its cost to the federal government and states, would seem to be logistically simple, requiring no more than a change in the criterion for medical necessity. It wouldn't require a change in legislation. It wouldn't require zoning changes. It wouldn't require governments to push back against NIMBY. It wouldn't require new investments in housing. It simply requires a recognition that hospital care is necessary for people who are actively struggling with uncontrolled psychotic symptoms and mood disorders, who have no other settings available to them, and who have no families able to care for them while their acute symptoms subside. The street cannot be treated as though it were a compassionate option.

LINK HOMELESS PEOPLE IN INSTITUTIONS TO HOUSING AND SERVICES

Since many homeless people show up in emergency rooms, inpatient units, and the correctional system, these institutions would seem to be logical places to link them to supportive housing. It would certainly seem like an obvious alternative to the current practice of dumping them onto the streets with no source of support, only to find them back again at these expensive medical and penal institutions a few days later. Below are some of the interventions that are crucial to changing this, although, again, all of them require an increased availability of housing for homeless people who are mentally ill:

- ACT teams or individual case managers should be linked with people who are about to be discharged from hospitals or released from jail.
- Media attention and public pressure should be brought to bear on the Joint Commission to enforce its requirement that hospitals safely discharge their patients when their emergency room and inpatient stays are completed. It holds that patients treated for mental illness and substance abuse should be released to appropriate housing and services, not sent to emergency shelters and the street.
- Public pressure should be focused on the Department of Health and Human Services for its failure to enforce its own Medicaid and Medicare standards, which require hospitals to prepare a discharge plan for those needing posthospital services, arrange for the initial implementation of the plan, and transfer or refer patients to appropriate facilities.
- Those states that have, as a matter of statute, or managed care contracts, outlawed discharges to the streets (e.g., Massachusetts) should be compelled in court to enforce these provisions.
- States should create zero-tolerance standards for hospital discharges to shelters or the streets, and class-action litigation should be used to require states to enforce these standards.

As described earlier, one of the reasons that homelessness has not decreased is governments' unwillingness to take steps to prevent it, even if certain programs have demonstrated that it was possible to do so. One of the most glaring failures of governments is their inattention to children who have experienced adverse childhood events, some of whom have been placed in foster care. As mentioned earlier, as many as 50 percent of the homeless population were once in foster care. Governments need to make much more serious and concerted efforts to help these children:

- Emotional support and counseling should be given to them as soon as they have been identified as coming from abusive or neglectful families.
- Better screening of potential foster care families is a must if these children are not going to be retraumatized by their foster care families.
- Foster care families should be given support and counseling particularly because the children they are responsible for have suffered the double traumas that have occurred in their families of origin and then of being removed from them.
- Counseling, support, and substance abuse treatment, rather than an exclusive reliance on medications, should be provided for children showing behavioral disturbances.
- Vocational guidance should be given to help these youth develop employable skills.
- As they age out of the foster care system, case management and linkage to housing and jobs must be provided in

order to reduce the number of youth who become homeless immediately upon leaving foster care and for years following this. There is simply no excuse for society to abandon them when they leave foster care.

- Given that extending foster care to twenty-one-year-olds appears to reduce the risk of homelessness, at least over the short term, states that have not already done so should consider passing legislation that would allow youths to remain in foster care until their twenty-first birthday (Dworsky et al., 2013).

THE LEGAL SYSTEM

The legal system has played an important role in mental health treatment with mixed positive and negative consequences. On one hand, it has protected the civil rights of people who in a bygone era would have been unreasonably admitted against their will to state hospitals and with no public defender in sight. On the other hand, it has unwittingly added to the number of mentally ill people on the street and in jail.

CHANGE THE CRITERIA FOR GRAVE DISABILITY

Currently the grave disability standard under which a judge can order a patient into inpatient treatment reads as follows: "Grave disability: A condition in which a person, as a result of a mental health disorder, is unable to provide for his or her basic personal needs for food, clothing, or shelter" (Southern

California Psychiatric Society, 2021). Judges have often surrendered their common sense when defining who is and isn't able to provide for his or her basic personal needs. Scrounging in trash barrels for food does not qualify as providing for the need for food, nor does having nothing but rags and walking around the streets half-naked qualify as providing clothing, nor does sleeping on the streets qualify for providing shelter. Yet as long as a person seems able to dig scraps out of garbage cans, find clothes however torn and threadbare, and find a sidewalk to sleep on, judges by and large do not define this person as being gravely disabled. But common sense dictates that these people should clearly be characterized as gravely disabled. Surely legislatures in enacting involuntary treatment legislation did not have such a restrictive interpretation in mind. Perhaps adding the word "safety" as a basic personal need would make the case clear. Until then, judges should use their common sense when deciding who is gravely disabled. Otherwise, they will continue to throw very disabled people back on the streets before they have been adequately treated and their needs for safety, shelter, food, and clothes provided for.

EXPAND THE USE OF COURT-ORDERED ASSISTED OUTPATIENT TREATMENT

In 2000 New York State enacted what became known as Kendra's Law. This was followed by the passage of one that is similar in California, known as Laura's Law. These laws allow courts, after extensive due process, to require a narrow group of chronically symptomatic individuals with serious mental illness who have past histories of multiple arrests, incarcerations, or hospitalizations and who refuse treatment voluntarily to accept outpatient treatment as a condition for living in the community. The goal of treatment is the prevention of relapse or deterioration that would likely result in serious harm to the patient or others were such treatment not ordered by the court.

One of the interesting developments that occurred in California in 2022 was a proposal from the governor and legislature to establish a special civil court, the Community Assistance, Recovery, and Empowerment (CARE) Court, to help as many as 12,000 severely mentally ill people who refuse outpatient treatment and are likely to deteriorate and harm themselves or others without it. The statute, which has been well described elsewhere and is broadly modeled after Kendra's and Laura's Laws, gives the CARE Court the authority to require mentally ill people who meet the criteria to accept treatment and housing against their will and fine counties if they fail to provide them. The court's authority to levy such fines may be as crucial to the success of this initiative as its authority to compel people into outpatient treatment.

Of note is the fact that the legislation allowing courts to commit this group of people to treatment on an outpatient basis has generated intense opposition from organizations such as the American Civil Liberties Union, which argue it will violate the civil rights of the people under court order. Their arguments are misguided.

- Argument 1: Court-ordered outpatient treatment deprives people of their freedom. This is true, but allowing them to deteriorate on the street without housing and services, even if these are involuntary, often leads to a much greater deprivation of freedom than when they are involuntarily placed in hospitals, jails, and long-term care facilities.

- Argument 2: The state shouldn't force people to accept services but should offer them voluntarily. Yes, a voluntary process would be preferable, but if people were cognitively able and willing to accept services voluntarily, they would do so and there would be no need for a coercive proposal. These people are so sick and have lost so much contact with reality, they can't take advantage of their civil rights. What rights can these people who are desperately poor, unhoused, unsafe, and hallucinating really take advantage of—the right to defecate on the street, to scrounge through garbage cans for food, to sleep in the freezing rain? These are tragedies, not rights.

- Argument 3: The CARE Court legislation would allow the most seriously disturbed people to cut in front of the line for services. While true, this is exactly what the proposal is designed to do. Unfair? No. These people have historically been left without services by housing providers and landlords, who are incentivized to provide housing to those with more resources and fewer problems. Absent this proposal, they will inevitably remain without services. However, many of the people willing to accept services voluntarily will still be eligible for a share of the $17.9 billion of new legislatively appropriated resources for low-cost affordable housing over the next decade.

- Argument 4: Voluntary services are more effective than involuntary services. The research is mixed, but in any event, the argument is irrelevant because this group of people won't accept voluntary services. A rigorous study by Duke University of Kendra's Law—New York's version of outpatient commitment—demonstrated that when compared to the three years prior to their participation in the program, 74 percent fewer experienced homelessness, 77 percent fewer experienced psychiatric hospitalizations, 83 percent fewer experienced arrests, and 87 percent fewer experienced incarceration. Self-harm attempts and substance abuse decreased by about half. Moreover, participants' perceptions were positive, with 81 percent saying the program had helped them get and stay well and 90 percent saying that the program had helped them take medication (Treatment Advocacy Center, n.d.). Clearly, clients subject to court-ordered treatment either didn't believe that their rights were violated by the process or believed that the benefits they received vastly outweighed any such violation.

- Argument 5: The CARE Court proposal is too expensive. This is untrue when it is compared to the cost of leaving people on the street. Supportive housing and treatment cost half of what it costs to leave a person unhoused. Homelessness is expensive, primarily due to the cost of police, transportation to the hospital, emergency room treatment, inpatient hospitalization, jail, long-term care in subacute psychiatric facilities, conservatorship, court appearances, and the public works staff who must clean up feces and needles on the street.

In summary, the arguments offered by opponents, however well intentioned, fail on all counts. While agreeing that this group of mentally ill people deserve help, opponents offer no realistic alternative. Yet without one, they consign these people to a continuation of their suffering, high mortality, constant dangers to their health and safety, and risks of much more severe restrictions on their liberty through long-term involuntary institutionalization in hospitals and jail. This legislation is important for the mentally ill in California, and since many other states are likely to follow its lead, California's CARE Court legislation is likely to set a necessary example for the nation.

PUT AN END TO THE PRACTICE OF CRIMINALIZING HOMELESSNESS

States and cities must put an end to the practice of systematically criminalizing homeless people for behaviors that are often necessary to survive on the streets. It is nothing short of cruel that governments, by their policies and actions, keep people homeless in the first place and then punish them for their lack of homes in the second place by citing or jailing them for lying on the streets, panhandling, jaywalking, loitering, sharing food, and other so-called nuisance behaviors. Instead of jail, these people should be provided with treatment and homes, which would almost certainly reduce the likelihood of engaging in these behaviors.

Given the number of people with mental disorders in jails and prisons, the entire legal system as it relates to the mentally ill needs to be rethought. This includes a reform of those laws and ordinances that punish people for their mental illness and homelessness, the ways that criminal laws are enforced, the treatment that is provided to people in the correctional system, and the creation of postrelease planning and services. Counties, which generally operate the jail systems, must stop the practices of jailing mentally ill people for nuisance crimes, failing to provide adequate treatment when they are incarcerated, and dumping them from jail onto the street once their sentences have been completed with no money, no place to live, and no treatment. If society's goal is to reduce the likelihood that mentally ill people will recommit crimes and be back in the correctional system, then they should be provided with real treatment when they are sentenced and housing and services when they are released. The present system simply sets them up for failure and recidivism.

WHAT NOT TO DO

A discussion of solutions would not be complete without some language describing what should not be done, especially when certain pseudosolutions are proposed and implemented that have little chance of success but are so seductive that they become the go-to interventions of certain cities.

In 2022, New York City mayor Eric Adams, reacting to recent incidents of violence by mentally ill people, announced a plan purporting to deal with the homeless crisis in the city. Using an approach that has failed in the past, the mayor directed the police to involuntarily remove mentally ill people from the city's streets and hospitalize those who putatively cannot care for themselves.

This is a pseudosolution that relies on expensive hospitals to compensate for the city's lack of outpatient treatment and supported housing. It will fail just as its predecessors have failed.

Why? For these reasons:

- The city does not have enough psychiatric hospital beds to treat current patients, much less accommodate a new influx of people, even if the New York governor makes good on her promise to add 150 beds in the future (Neber, 2023). Ironically, the state and city have been on a campaign to shut down psychiatric beds for years. The situation was aggravated further during the COVID-19 pandemic, when many of the remaining beds were "repurposed" for COVID patients; 415 of these beds are still closed (Geringer-Sameth, 2022). The mayor's proposal will aggravate this bed shortage further, and psychiatric emergency rooms will become even more overcrowded than they are at present.
- As is the case throughout the country, there are insufficient outpatient treatment services and a dearth of housing for patients when they leave the hospital. Without treatment and housing, people will either remain in the hospital even when hospital care is no longer needed or be forced out of the hospital prematurely with no suitable place to go. Although the mayor promised that people will not be discharged unless follow-up services are in place, this pledge is naïve on two counts and will prove impossible to carry out. First, since these services don't exist in sufficient numbers, people would be forced to stay in the

hospital beyond the time they need to, further reducing the availability of beds for new patients. Second, the courts cannot legally prolong people's involuntary hospitalization when they no longer meet the statutory requirements for coercive treatment. These patients will be discharged by the courts whether or not treatment and housing are available to them.

- Hospital beds are expensive and should be utilized selectively when people need this level of care. They should not be squandered on people who might not have needed intensive and coercive treatment had the city provided housing and treatment for them before they deteriorated and needed hospitalization.

- A policy that fails to address the real dearth of housing and services will simply accelerate the revolving door to and from psychiatric emergency rooms in the city. Of the 7,426 supportive housing applicants in the last fiscal year, just 1,224 were ultimately approved for housing (Evelly, 2022). Mental health clinics are booked for months out, and many of them lack sufficient case management services on which severely mentally ill patients depend. The mayor's proposal does nothing to solve these problems. It will just move people around the system from the streets into hospitals and back to the streets.

- Involuntary hospitalization represents the most restrictive treatment when the availability of outpatient treatment and supportive housing could have prevented the need for this in many cases. Involuntary hospitalization should be used for those people who are frankly dangerous to themselves or others. There is a real possibility that the mayor's vague criteria for whom the police can apprehend and hospitalize involuntarily are likely to be challenged in court for this reason alone. One wonders whether the mayor has a plan B.

Mayor Adams should be commended for wanting to do something about people with serious mental illness, but history has demonstrated that policies and plans that are poorly conceived do not help and can make situations much worse for both the mentally ill and society. His proposal may reduce the political heat that recent violent incidents have engendered but will not solve the problem of untreated mental illness in the city that generated public pressure in the first place.

As noted earlier, the historical context is important. Failed policies are nothing new to the mentally ill. Over the years, mentally ill people have been pushed around by one disastrous government policy after another. In the early nineteenth century, they were moved from jails and almshouses to asylums, which were then allowed to deteriorate into large, overcrowded, underfunded state hospitals. Many patients lived there because they were poor, had difficulty functioning, and had nowhere else to live.

Dumped out of these facilities without follow-up in the late twentieth century, many were forced to live on the streets with no housing and no treatment. Some ultimately found their way into poor, shoddy SROs, but 60 percent of these settings were closed between 1975 and 1995 as a result of gentrification, largely promoted by the city, which actually gave tax breaks to developers to help them in this conversion (Jacobs, 2021). People ended up on the streets again.

Although New York City mayor Bill de Blasio worked with private developers to build 160,000 housing units of various levels, most of these are completely out of reach for those who need housing most. As of 2020, some 25 million applications had been submitted for roughly 40,000 units (Jacobs, 2021).

Responding to the terms of a lawsuit, the city created shelters for homeless people, but without alternative forms of housing, the number of shelter beds increased almost exponentially. Approximately 64,000 people now remain homeless in these facilities, often having to wait months and sometimes years for an apartment they can afford (Simone, 2019).

The average stay in shelters rose to 401 days for single adults in 2018, but many people stay much longer (Simone, 2019). Many shelters are so overcrowded and dangerous that some people shun them altogether, preferring to take their chances on the streets. It is a subset of this group of people whom the mayor is now proposing to involuntarily hospitalize. But isn't this where we started two centuries ago—hospitalizing many mentally ill people because they were very poor and had nowhere else to go?

Hospitalization has never been the solution to inadequate housing and outpatient treatment. Although the city is taking steps to increase the amount of affordable housing, these initiatives are and have always been so puny, so inadequate in scope, that they will never come close to meeting the need. If 65,000 mentally ill people are stuck in shelters, how are a few new hospital beds and a few thousand planned new housing units and treatment slots going to solve their homelessness?

The city may claim bragging rights that it is at least doing *something*, but the mayor's plan won't come close to solving the problem. People who are swept off the street by the police and taken to hospitals will find themselves back on the street after their brief stay in hospitals, and the cycle will begin all over again.

The tragedy is that we know how to solve these problems: create enough supported housing and outpatient treatment services so that people don't have to languish in shelters or on the streets. So why has Mayor Adams offered a proposal that ignores this solution and thus misses the mark so badly? Possibly because it gives the appearance of doing something while costing very little. Nor does it require any real action on the part of his administration. Offload the problem to the police and hospitals and be done with it.

The mayor's new policy is a mirage, not a solution.

A Tale of Two Cities

In considering possible solutions to homelessness, it is enlightening to contrast the experience of two cities, San Francisco and Trieste, Italy. The former has an enormous number of homeless mentally ill people. The latter has none. What accounts for this difference, and what we can we learn from it?

Trieste, a homogeneous, largely middle-class city of 200,000 citizens, has no poverty, very little drug abuse, no crime, and families that accept and exercise responsibility for their disabled relatives. Its mental health system is supported by a universal right to health care and housing (Portacolone et al., 2015). San Francisco, with a population of 874,000, is ethnically diverse and has a large population of poor and disabled people, stark disparities in the income and wealth of its citizens, and the largest per capita number of homeless people in the United States. In the last eight years, San Francisco surpassed every other city in the country as the locality with the highest income gap between rich and poor residents. The existence of such a large class of extremely poor and disabled people creates a situation in which the demand for human services is intense; thus, the large number of mentally ill people in the city are forced to compete for these services with other disadvantaged groups. As described earlier, there is no right to either housing or health care, much less mental health care, in the United States, resulting in a social safety net that is underfunded, thin, and full of holes.

In addition to these severe differences in the demographic, social, and economic characteristics of the two cities, the contrast in the way that deinstitutionalization was carried out and the underlying principles guiding this process could not have been greater. Deinstitutionalization in the United States was motivated primarily by fiscal incentives rather than concerns about the resulting quality of life of patients who were discharged. The process in Trieste was inspired by the conviction that the values, conditions, hierarchical structure of the mental hospital, and the segregation of patients from society were antithetical to their basic rights as human beings, and moreover, contributed to their symptoms. Only closure of the hospital and its replacement with a system that embodied fundamentally different values could transform their lives. Bringing about this transformation was the guiding vision for the process of closing the mental hospital and creating an alternative to it.

In addition to the difference in the motivations behind the deinstitutionalization movement in the two cities were the political contexts within which it took place. The mentally ill in the United States had almost no allies in the political arena, a fact that left them vulnerable to the economic imperatives of the state governments that were driving the process. The result was first a wholesale abandonment of discharged people and then the creation of an underfunded nonsystem of "care." The process was one of geographic translocation rather than real transformation. The community service movement, in so far as it developed at all, was crippled from the start. And even the advent of community mental health centers failed to provide people with the treatment and support they needed because the mission and priorities of these services were hijacked by much less disturbed and disabled people, most of whom had never been patients in state hospitals.

In Trieste, the process of deinstitutionalization was supported by political movements led by students, women, and workers who were demanding relief from their own experience of oppression, a fact that enabled them to identify with and ultimately adopt the cause of the mentally ill as their allies. Their support was vital to preserving and reallocating funds for the new community system, protecting its radical values, and ensuring that it kept its focus on the patients who had previously been inmates in the mental hospital.

It was inevitable that the two community systems that developed in the wake of deinstitutionalization would be starkly different, given the contrast in the forces that led to their creation, the political context in which they were born, and the amount of funding that the two received. Even the etiology of mental illness and its symptoms were viewed differently by the two systems. Underpinning the community mental health system that developed in the United States was a model of care that was primarily medical and tended to view clients as a collection of their symptoms and biological needs. The goals of the community system were generally restricted to the amelioration of these symptoms rather than being concerned with the totality of their human needs.

Due to the leadership and vision of the radical psychiatrist Franco Basaglia, who led the deinstitutionalization movement in Trieste, the community system that developed there viewed people with mental disorders first and foremost as human beings with all the rights and privileges of other members of society—a foundational belief with profound implications for the closure of the mental hospital and creation of the new community system. Basaglia argued that they had the right to be different without being stigmatized as deviant or dangerous, which had historically been used by society to dehumanize them in institutions. While he didn't deny the existence of biological factors in the etiology of mental illness, Basaglia argued that the individual's symptoms were aggravated by the coercive, deadening, impoverished conditions of the mental hospital, which encouraged regression, passivity, and demoralization. If in closing the hospital, its values, degrading conditions, and hierarchical structure were not challenged, these characteristics would, he believed, simply be reproduced in the community. The dehumanization of patients would then be transferred along with the locus of their care to the community system.

Through the deinstitutionalization process, he sought to "place the person rather than his illness at the center of the mental health system" and thereby restore the person's humanity (Okin, 2020). Individuals, he argued, had the right to make choices about their lives, and the design of the mental health system had to facilitate this. As a corollary to the right to make choices, people were to be free from every type of coercion to which they had historically been subjected—seclusion and restraint, involuntary commitment to even the most humane hospitals, and incarceration in jails.

Beyond their civil right to liberty, individuals were to be helped to exercise their social, political, and economic rights as well. Housing, health care, and an adequate income were to be accessible to them, which, along with the involvement of their families, would provide a strong social safety net, on top of which the new mental health system was to be created. Without the fulfillment of these rights, no mental health system could be successful and would, of necessity, be forced to restrict itself exclusively to addressing only their most basic biological needs.

Their other human needs would be ignored for lack of time, money, and inspiration. A strong mental health department as the governance of the new community system was to be created to protect its values, integrate its components, assure continuity of care, and provide adequate and flexible funding necessary to support such a novel community system.

The results of these foundational principles and the advocacy they inspired are dramatic and can be seen today in Trieste. The mental hospital is virtually closed and instead provides housing for five hundred "guests" who live independently on the grounds of the hospital, which itself is located in the heart of the city. Crucial to the therapeutic process and vital to recovery are individuals' full inclusion into the fabric of society, a principle that challenged the prevailing and longstanding medical, social, and legal justifications for the segregation of people with mental illness. To accomplish this and to animate their rights to full citizenship, the mental health system encourages their active engagement in the social life of the community and supports the exercise of their rights to decent housing, jobs that are integrated into the employment structure of the community, and involvement in political parties and religious and civic organizations. Many participate in the creation of life projects, jobs, and social relationships and are actively engaged in public life. People with mental illness work and live alongside the rest of the community, almost never requiring acute hospitalization or long-term institutional care.

If people need emergency care, they receive it not primarily in hospitals but in mental health centers, which are housed in a more normal, homelike, nonmedical environment. The very close contact the centers have with their clients makes unrecognized deterioration with no advance warning the exception rather than the rule. People are not allowed to fall apart without this triggering the active, comprehensive intervention of staff, which results in acute episodes that are far less severe and dramatic than they would be were staff not so involved in their daily lives. This partially accounts for the very low need for acute hospitalization. Symptoms that do become the center of attention are managed not exclusively with medication but through changing clients' position from what might otherwise be a state of passive dependence to one of active and engaged participation with the staff. The roles of psychiatrists and other staff have been modified to promote social equality with clients and permit their inclusion as an active part of the treatment team. Clinicians' attention is less centered on clients' symptoms and basic survival and more so on helping them create lives with aspirations, intentionality, and purpose. Support for people's families is a critical intervention since so many people live with and depend on their relatives. Coercion of any type is rarely required, involuntary commitment has been eliminated, incarceration of mentally ill people in penal institutions has largely been abandoned except in rare instances, and homelessness does not exist (Mezzina, 2014).

Complex social systems have multiple and diverse features, which makes it difficult to identify with precision the factors that have made Trieste so successful in preventing homelessness. Is it due to

- The underlying social and economic conditions that prevail there (e.g., the absence of a very poor class of people, the relatively small disparities in wealth, a homogeneous population, the existence of adequate housing, or other elements of a robust social safety net)?

- The way that deinstitutionalization was carried out, the political support it received, and the funding that thus became available?
- The fact that housing is provided for guests on the grounds of the old mental hospital, thus obviating the need for as much housing in the community?
- The core beliefs and values that undergird the community system and animate the ways it operates, its belief that peoples' problems and symptoms are not primarily the result of biological factors or their own intrinsic shortcomings but are contributed to in major ways by the society in which they live?
- Its focus on the totality of its clients' needs, not just their symptoms and needs for basic survival?
- The founders' conviction that people with mental disorders have the same rights to thrive and be integrated into society that others do?
- The extensive efforts the staff make in the city to destigmatize people with mental illness?

Perhaps each of these factors has played a role. In our search for the factors that led to the development of the Trieste mental health system, it is relevant to note that its success has not been replicated, even in the rest of Italy, where the very precious conditions that permitted its development do not exist.

Because of Trieste's relatively unique demographic characteristics, it would be easy to argue that its success in caring for people with mental illness and its lack of homelessness is not generalizable but solely attributable to the fact that it was developed in a virtual petri dish, devoid of the destructive contaminants that affect most other societies. The importance of these characteristics is unarguable, but it is possible and indeed likely that the success of Trieste's mental health system also stems from the fundamentally different way it views mental illness and those who suffer from it. In this respect, Trieste has much to teach us, which is why I described its mental health system in such detail.

As noted above, and in contrast to Trieste, mental illness in the United States is viewed primarily as a biological phenomenon. Social and economic influences on the particular expression of its symptoms are minimized. In this sense, homelessness among the mentally ill is attributed to malformations in their DNA rather than to the destructive way we view and treat people with mental disorders. When we see someone who is homeless and raving on the street, we tend to think, "Well, this is because he's mentally ill and biologically compromised." End of story. We don't tend to recognize that it may be the way society has stigmatized his disorder rather than its intrinsic characteristics that also accounts for his behavior and homelessness. In fact, while homelessness may evoke public sympathy as an abstract matter, homeless mentally ill individuals seem to elicit revulsion when we see them in the flesh.

The social stigma that underlies this reaction and its political and economic consequences have been the major culprits in this tragic drama throughout the twists and turns of history. If people are viewed as less than human, it is easy to marginalize, segregate, and place them in coercive institutions. It is easy to deprive them of food, shelter, and other resources. It is easy to allow them to become homeless and to enact policies that make this virtually inevitable. It is precisely because our attitudes lead to the policies, priorities, budgets, and actions of governments that make them so crucial. While other factors play important roles, the independent contribution of our attitudes to the prevalence of homelessness in the United States cannot be overstated.

SUMMARY OF SOLUTIONS

The solutions to the homeless crisis in the United States must address the factors that lead to mentally ill people being pushed onto the streets. These include the following:

PROVIDE AFFORDABLE HOUSING FOR MENTALLY ILL HOMELESS OR THOSE AT RISK

This is the sine qua non of any comprehensive solution to the problem of homelessness. Governments must stop nibbling around the edges of the problem and create enough housing to help people both already on the street and those at risk of becoming homeless.

- *Create supportive housing*—People with mental illness often have severe and debilitating symptoms. Without either clinical staff on site or readily available to support and treat them, many will not be able to maintain themselves in their housing.

- *Utilize a housing-first approach in determining access to housing*—Expecting homeless people with mental illness and/or substance abuse disorders to either take their medications or give up their addictions has proven unrealistic. The dangers, stresses, and distractions of street life simply make this impossible. Housing must be provided as a precondition of stabilizing their psychiatric and substance abuse disorders and must be implemented as the first intervention, not the last.
- *Increase the number and quality of shelters*—As long as shelters are either unavailable or viewed by people as dangerous, demeaning, and stressful, they won't be viewed by many people as a realistic alternative to the street. Temporary shelters should be created as just that: temporary. This will be realistic only when sufficient permanent housing is available. Otherwise, people either won't use them or if compelled, as in New York City, will be stuck in them for years. It is important to recognize that shelters are not homes. They are four walls and a roof shared by strangers.

CREATE AN ENLIGHTENED COMPREHENSIVE COMMUNITY TREATMENT SYSTEM

Without creating a different kind of community system than that which exists today, we are always going to be hampered in our efforts to help people leave the streets and stably remain in housing. Instead, we need to create a comprehensive system that holistically treats all members of the community in a productive manner and includes the following elements:

- *Develop a service system of adequately paid, well-trained case managers and assertive community treatment teams—*Without this clinical staff, many homeless people will not be housed, and those that already are will not be able to remain there. Their symptoms will sabotage their tenure.

- *Increase the availability and acceptability of substance abuse treatment—*It is not reasonable to expect people to give up an addiction under the best of circumstances. In many places, it is the worst of circumstances they encounter. Clinicians need skill, understanding, patience, and a willingness to accept inevitable failures and setbacks to do this work.

- *Develop opportunities for vocational training and supportive employment—*Given the importance of work as a source of structure, support, self-esteem, and income, it is crucial that these opportunities be created. It is also important for peoples' psychological development that they pay for the services they receive to the extent they can. Finally, it might reduce the resentment the general public has toward people they regard as freeloaders.

- *Increase the availability of psychiatric beds in general hospitals and reduce the financially driven pressure to discharge people to the streets—*The number of psychiatric beds in general hospitals across the country has declined dramatically over the last two decades. Unless more beds are created, even if these are temporary until housing is expanded, people who desperately need inpatient treatment will be denied admission and pushed out of hospitals prematurely.

- *Develop a tracking system to identify homeless mentally ill people and their needs—*Without this, interventions will be scattershot, and the whole system will be flying blind.

- *Link homeless people from hospitals and jails to housing and services*—Unless this is done, people will end up on the streets in the very conditions that precipitated their admission to these facilities in the first place.
- *Provide services to high-risk youth*—Many homeless mentally ill people experienced neglect or abuse as children, and as many as 50 percent of homeless mentally ill people are graduates of the foster care system. Improvements in services for high-risk youth are critical if the inflow to the streets is to be slowed. Unless these measures are taken, it will be very difficult to reduce the prevalence of homelessness. For every person we take off the streets, another will take his or her place.

MODERNIZE CERTAIN ASPECTS OF THE LEGAL SYSTEM

Although often overlooked, the legal system is an intimate part of mental health treatment and has a vital part to play in reducing homelessness. By fixing how we create, enact, and uphold laws, we can actually help the people they're intended to support. The following steps can do just that:

- *Change the interpretation of grave disability*—The courts have done incalculable harm through their unrealistically narrow definition of what constitutes grave disability. People who are in no condition to leave involuntary hospital treatment are thrown back onto the streets by courts that profess they are guarding peoples' civil rights.

- *Expand the use of court-ordered assisted outpatient treatment—* This has proven to dramatically reduce the incidence of homelessness, hospitalization, and incarceration. It should be expanded in states beyond New York and California where it was piloted.
- *Put an end to the practice of criminalizing homelessness—* Incarcerating homeless people for nuisance crimes is generally as useless and expensive as it is cruel. The resources wasted on this should be redirected to provide the housing and services that people need to get off the streets so they are less likely to recommit these crimes.

FINAL THOUGHTS

As we conclude this section on solutions to homelessness of people with mental illness, we need to return to the question of whether it is possible to overcome or circumvent the forces that have created it in the first place. The success of Trieste in creating a humane mental health system and the absence of homelessness in that city, although multidetermined, and the other successes I have cited above suggest that the problem is solvable but only if sufficient political will to do so can be mobilized. For this to happen, we need to recognize that people with severe mental illness on the street are more like us than different. We need to recognize that these people whom we tend to blame or fear were once children, often compromised by their biological vulnerability from birth and born into families that were frequently dysfunctional, abusive, or neglectful. Their experiences as children severely traumatized them. Many were ripped out of these families and placed into strange and unfamiliar ones, some of whom were as hurtful as the families from which they were removed. Thus, they developed the only coping mechanisms they could, usually without any treatment or support, and their trauma and the destructive strategies they developed to deal with it often led to pervasive problems in executive functioning, social relationships, and school. During adolescence many turned to drugs to dull their emotional pain, fell behind in school, and entered adulthood with no employable skills and with no ability to pull their lives together.

A combination of these problems and the way society views their psychiatric symptoms all but made it impossible to find a job and thus a home. Without any financial or emotional support, the street was the only place they could go. If we could remember that they encountered more pain, more trauma, and more obstacles than the rest of us can barely imagine, we might feel enough compassion to help them, most importantly through the political sphere.

However desirable this may be, the solution to homelessness cannot be left to hang from the slender thread of those who feel compassion for these people. Even if we've become inured to the suffering of mentally ill people on the street, the fact is that none of us can escape being affected by their presence in our midst. As much as we might look away when we pass them, they inevitably touch us, even if subliminally. Even if we don't feel sympathy for them, we can't help but feel disturbed and uneasy in the face of such human misery. Unless we live in a complete bubble, we cannot hide from evidence of their poverty, such as the fact that they have no place to sleep or bathe or go to the toilet. We can't avoid their needles or feces on the street. We can't hide from their shopping carts. We can't entirely block out their delusional ravings. Like it or not, we are forced to confront the problem, and blaming them for their misery will not help us escape it. We might then conclude that we would all be better off if the people we pass on the street were also better off.

Whether our motivation springs from compassion, angry self-interest, or a wish to avoid these people altogether, most of us on both sides of the political spectrum will ultimately be moved to take action and demand of our political leaders that they stop wringing their hands, give up their addiction to halfway measures, and quit tiptoeing around the edges of the problem. Of course, dividing citizens into these two camps is admittedly an oversimplification, a heuristic device, for most of us find ourselves in both camps at one time or another. Especially during this period of such intense political polarization and rancor, we need to enlist and mobilize both groups of people, whatever their motivation, not just one or the other. When politicians recognize that both groups could imperil their political futures unless they do something meaningful, they will take action to solve the problem. And when they do, people who are homeless and mentally ill will, for the first time in their lives, get what they never had before—a fighting chance.

CONCLUSION

As the reader turns the last page of this book, I hope he or she thinks, "I suppose the people portrayed here are not so different from me. Maybe if I were as biologically vulnerable, if I had suffered one trauma after another as a child, if I were poor and didn't have a source of income or the means to get it, if I didn't have a family to stay with, I too might be living on the street. And if I lived on the street, I guess I'd look pretty dirty, and I might smell, and I'd probably be lugging around a cart, because where else would I keep my things? And if I slept on the street, exposed to the weather and the dirt and the grime, of course I'd get skin infections and look like I had some kind of pox. Of course my teeth would become abscessed and I'd have to get them pulled, particularly if I couldn't get Medicaid to fix them in a more sophisticated (and expensive) way. And of course I'd look weird and unapproachable. And if I didn't have any food and was hungry enough, I might dive into dumpsters for half-eaten sandwiches, grab meals at soup kitchens, steal, or panhandle.

"And perhaps if I had to face all this, day after day, and if I had suffered one loss after another, some admittedly by my own hand, I would be bored or miserable enough to dabble in drugs. And if this took the sting out of life, maybe I would do more than dabble. Maybe I'd get hooked. And if I did, I doubt I'd want to spend whatever handouts I was able to get on housing. Yeah, looked at in a certain way, I get all that."

If we could hear beyond the silence and see beyond the symptoms of the homeless mentally ill, we might be able to perceive the ways we are the same, not just the ways we are different.

We'd be able to see that we all get cold when the temperature drops, wet and uncomfortable when it rains on us, and exhausted when we haven't slept. We'd be able to see that we all get hungry for food, affection, esteem, money—something. We'd have to acknowledge that we all have feelings, needs, and vulnerabilities; that we're all trying to make sense of our worlds; and that we all screw up and do things that make bad situations worse, take the wrong path, or fall off the horse and have trouble getting back on.

And if we understood all this, we might feel more connected to the people we now shun. We might identify with their predicaments. We might offer them more understanding and less blame. We might choose to include them in, rather than exclude them from, the spheres of life that are open to the rest of us. We might be more willing to share with them than withhold from them, and feel less resentful doing so.

And if our willingness to share extended to the political realm, we might make different decisions as a society. We might be more willing to enact legislation that would provide mentally ill people with decent housing, clothes, food, dental care, and mental health treatment. This, in turn, would make it easier for us to see what we have in common with them. Seeing them as fully human, we might also be less likely to segregate and punish them. We might conclude that they are entitled to a life of dignity, simply because they are human.

ACKNOWLEDGMENTS

To my sweetheart, Cynthia Broughton, who helped me in more ways than I can enumerate throughout the writing of this second edition.

Thank you to Dorothy Dundas, whose life story exemplifies courage and compassion and whose wise consultation and encouragement were vital throughout this project.

To my photography mentor, Donald Kennedy, who accompanied me on the street in the early days of the project and taught me everything I came to know about photography.

To my dear companion Steve Bearman, who provided me with the friendship, support, and insight I needed to face down my demons in writing this book.

To my friends Larry and Ellie Lurie and Steve Walsh for their tireless and extremely helpful review of several drafts of this second edition.

To my daughter, Laura, and my son, Justin, who reviewed draft after draft, provided me with crucial feedback, and never gave up on my vision for this project.

To my sister, Nicki, my brother-in-law, Gerard, my brother, Ken, and my sister-in-law, Elaine, who have supported and encouraged me over the years, who lifted my spirits when they had plummeted, and who always believed that this book had something of importance to say.

And to my mother and father, whose values, courage, and willingness to stand up for what they believed set me on a path for life.

REFERENCES

Anderson S., Boe T., & Smith S. (1988). Homeless women. *Journal of Women and Social Work*, *3*(2), 62–70.

Beer, T. (2020, October 8). Top 1% of U.S. households hold 15 times more wealth than bottom 50% combined. *Forbes*. https://www.forbes.com/sites/tommybeer/2020/10/08/top-1-of-us-households-hold-15-times-more-wealth-than-bottom-50-combined/

Bellisario, J., Weinberg, M., Mena, C., & Yang, L. (2016). *Solving the housing affordability crisis*. Bay Area Council Economic Institute. http://www.bayareaeconomy.org/files/pdf/BACEI_Housing_10_2016.pdf

Butterfield, F. (1999, July 12). Experts say study confirms prison's new role as mental hospital. *The New York Times*.

Callahan v. Carey, 42582/79. New York Superior Court, New York County (1979). https://www.escr-net.org/caselaw/2006/callahan-v-carey-no-79-42582-sup-ct-ny-county-cot-18-1979

CBS San Francisco. (2021, June 26). San Francisco rents on the rise amid reduced COVID restrictions: Return to office work. *CBS*. https://sanfrancisco.cbslocal.com/2021/06/26/san-francisco-rents-covid-19-on-rise-housing/

Children's Defense Fund. (2020). *The state of America's children: Child hunger and nutrition*. https://www.childrensdefense.org/policy/resources/soac-2020-child-hunger/

City and County of San Francisco. (2020). *City performance scorecards*. https://sfgov.org/scorecards/safety-net/homeless-population

Culhane, D. P., Metraux, S., & Hadley, T. (2002). Public service reductions associated with placement of homeless persons with severe mental illness in supportive housing. *Housing Policy Debates*, *13*(1), 107–163. https://repository.upenn.edu/spp_papers/65

Daily Hive Vancouver Staff. (2021, February 22). Here's what to expect from Vancouvers rental market this year. *Daily Hive*. https://dailyhive.com/vancouver/vancouver-rental-market-2021

DiPrinzio, H. (2019, December 24). City housing data drop: Longer shelter stays. More permanent housing. NYCHA rent collection lags. *City Limits.*

Ditton, P. (1999, July). *Mental health and treatment of inmates and probationers.* Bureau of Justice Statistics, Department of Justice.

Dronen, C. (n.d.) Aging out of the foster care statistics. *Finally Family Homes.* https://finallyfamilyhomes.org/the-problem/

Dworsky, A., Napolitano, L., & Courtney, M. (2013, December). Homelessness during the transition from foster care to adulthood. *American Journal of Public Health, 103*(S2), S318–323.

Edalati, H., Nicholls, T. L., Crocker, A. G., Roy, L., Somers, J. M., & Patterson, M. L. (2017). Adverse childhood experiences and the risk of criminal justice involvement and victimization among homeless adults with mental illness. *Psychiatric Services, 68*(12), 1288–1295. https://doi.org/10.1176/appi.ps.201600330

Editorial Board. (2019, January 30) It's already hard to get a Section 8 voucher: It's even harder to find a landlord willing to take it. *Los Angeles Times.* https://www.latimes.com/opinion/editorials/la-ed-section-8-discrimination-ban-20190130-story.html

Edwards, S. (2019, April 24). The push to make housing a human right comes to hot docs. *Now Toronto.* https://nowtoronto.com/movies/news-features/hot-docs-leilani-farha-push-housing

Evelly, J. (2022, September 9). City's Supportive housing remains out of reach for most applicants, data shows. *City Limits.* https://citylimits.org/2022/09/09/citys-supportive-housing-remains-out-of-reach-for-most-applicants-data-shows/

Geringer-Sameth, E. (2022, November 28). Despite state budget funding, little progress bringing psychiatric beds back into service. *Gotham Gazette.* https://www.gothamgazette.com/state/11696-ny-state-budget-little-progress-psychiatric-beds-hochul-adams

Grey, C., & Woodfine, L. (2019). *Voices of those with lived experiences of homelessness and adversity in Wales: Informing prevention and response.* Public Health Wales NHS Trust.

Hansen, S. (2020, June 5) Here's what the racial wealth gap in America looks like today. *Forbes.* https://www.forbes.com/sites/sarahhansen/2020/06/05/heres-what-the-racial-wealth-gap-in-america-looks-like-today/

Healy, P. (2017, June 8). The fundamental attribution error: What it is and how to avoid it. *Harvard Business School Online.* https://online.hbs.edu/blog/post/the-fundamental-attribution-error

Heslin, K., & Weiss, A. (2015, May) *Statistical Brief #189: Hospital readmissions involving psychiatric disorders, 2012.* Department of Health and Human Services. https://www.hcup-us.ahrq.gov/reports/statbriefs/sb189-Hospital-Readmissions-Psychiatric-Disorders-2012.jsp

Jacobs, K. (2021, June 24). It's time for New York City to bring back SROs. *New York Magazine.* https://www.curbed.com/2021/06/sro-hotels-nyc-bring-back.html

Jaffe, D. J. (n.d.) *Loopholes in Kendra's Law that need closing.* Mental Illness Policy Org. https://mentalillnesspolicy.org/kendras-law/kendras-law-improvements.html

Josefowitz, N. (2018, May 17). *The one stat that explains SF's street homeless crisis.* Medium. https://medium.com/@josefow/the-one-stat-that-explains-sfs-street-homeless-crisis-e863329ba8ed

Kieschnick, H. (2018) A cruel and unusual way to regulate the homeless. *Stanford Law Review, 70*(5), 1569.

King, M. L. Jr. (1958, February 8). *The gospel messenger, Out of the long night.* Official Organ of the Church of the Brethren. https://archive.org/details/gospelmessengerv107mors

Lamb, H., & Weinberger, L. (2005). The shift of psychiatric inpatient care from hospitals to jails and prisons. *Journal of the American Academy of Psychiatry and the Law, 33*(4), 529–534.

Lee, C. M., Mangurian, C., Tieu, L., Ponath, C., Guzman, D., & Kushel, M. (2016). Childhood adversities associated with poor adult mental health outcomes in older homeless adults: Results from the hope home study. *American Journal of Geriatric Psychiatry, 25*(2), 107–117.

Lipsitt, D., (2003, June). Psychiatry and the general hospital in an age of uncertainty. *World Psychiatry*, *2*(2), 87–92.

Lutkehaus, N. (2008). *Margaret Mead: The making of an American icon.* Princeton University Press.

McCarty, M., Perl, L., & Jones, K. (2019). *Overview of federal housing assistance programs and policy.* Congressional Research Service. https://crsreports.congress.gov/product/pdf/RL/RL34591

Mezzina, R. (2014). Community mental health in Trieste and beyond: An "open door-no restraint" system of care for recovery and citizenship. *Journal of Nervous and Mental Disease*, *202*(6), 440–445.

National Alliance to End Homelessness. (2017, February 17). *Ending chronic homelessness saves taxpayers money.* https://endhomelessness.org/resource/ending-chronic-homelessness-saves-taxpayers-money-2/

National Institute of Drug Abuse (2021, April 13). *Part 1: The connection between substance use disorders and mental illness.* https://www.drugabuse.gov/publications/research-reports/common-comorbidities-substance-use-disorders/part-1-connection-between-substance-use-disorders-mental-illness

Neber, J. (2023, January 10). Hochul dedicates $1B to address mental illness. *Crain's New York Business.* https://www.crainsnewyork.com/health-care/kathy-hochul-unveils-1b-plan-address-mental-illness-new-york

Official Journal at the European Communities. (2000, December 18). *Charter of Fundamental rights of the European Union.*

Okin, R. (2020). The Trieste model: Obstacles to replication in the United States. In T. Burns & J. Foot (Ed.), *Basaglia's International Legacy* (pp. 317–332). Oxford University Press.

Parilla, J. & Liu, S. (2018, March). Examining the local value of economic development incentives: Evidence from four U.S. cities. *Brookings Institution.* https://www.brookings.edu/wp-content/uploads/2018/02/report_examining-the-local-value-of-economic-development-incentives_brookings-metro_march-2018.pdf

Patterson, M., Moniruzzaman, A. & Somers, J. (2014, April). Setting the stage for chronic health problems: Cumulative childhood adversity among homeless adults with mental illness in Vancouver, British Columbia. *BMC Public Health, 14*(350). https://doi.org/10.1186/1471-2458-14-350

Portacolone E., Mezzina R., Shepherd-Hughes N., & Okin R., (2015). A tale of two cities: The exploration of the Trieste public psychiatry model in San Francisco. *Culture, Medicine and Psychiatry, 39*(4), 680–697.

Ray, J., & Gosling, F. (1982). Historical perspectives on the treatment of mental illness in the United States. *The Journal of Psychiatry and Law, 10*(2), 135–161. https://doi.org/10.1177/009318538201000203

Sadowski L., Kee R., VanderWeele T., & Buchanan D. (2009). Effect of a housing and case management program on emergency department visits and hospitalizations among chronically ill homeless adults: A randomized trial. *JAMA, 301*(17), 1771.

Sentencing Project. (2002, January). *Mentally ill offenders in the criminal justice system: An analysis and prescription.* https://www .sentencingproject.org/wp-content/uploads/2016/01/Mentally-Ill -Offenders-in-the-Criminal-Justice-System.pdf

Simone, J. (2019, March 21). *Homeless New Yorkers are spending more time in shelters than ever before.* Coalition for the Homeless. https://www .coalitionforthehomeless.org/todays-read-homeless-new-yorkers -are-spending-more-time-in-shelters-than-ever-before/

Southern California Psychiatric Society. (2021). *Grave disability, inadequately defined in California.* https://www.socalpsych .org/2020/11/grave-disability-inadequately-defined-in-california-2/

Torrey, F. (n.d.). *Criminalization of mental illness of people with severe psychiatric disorders.* Mental Illness Policy Org. https:// mentalillnesspolicy.org/consequences/criminalization.html

Treatment Advocacy Center. (n.d.). *First ten years with assisted outpatient treatment.* https://www.treatmentadvocacycenter.org/fixing-the-system /features-and-news/41-research-weekly-serious-mental-illness-and -rehospitalization-an-update

Treatment Advocacy Center. (2016a). *Serious mental illness prevalence in jails and prisons.* https://www.treatmentadvocacycenter.org/evidence-and-research/learn-more-about/3695

Treatment Advocacy Center. (2016b). *Released, relapsed, rehospitalized: Length of stay and readmission rates in state hospitals, a comparative survey.* https://www.TreatmentAdvocacyCenter.org/released-relapsed-rehospitalized

United States Department of Housing and Urban Development. (2016). *Homelessness prevention and rapid re-housing program (HPRP): Year three and final program summary.* https://files.hudexchange.info/resources/documents/HPRP-Year-3-Summary.pdf

United States Department of Housing and Urban Development. (2021). *The 2020 annual homeless assessment report (AHAR) to Congress.* https://www.huduser.gov/portal/sites/default/files/pdf/2020-AHAR-Part-1.pdf

INDEX

mental illness (*continued*)
    criminalization of, 222–225, 251, 286–287, 305
    deinstitutionalization and, 209–211, 249, 293–296
    development of, 18
    drug addiction and, 211–212
    general hospitals and, 218–220, 250, 277–278, 303
    homelessness and, 1, 3, 7–8, 18, 205
    inclusion and, 269–271
    mental hospitals and, 206–211
    public assistance and, 24–26, 213–214
    social stigma of, 32–33, 252, 300–301
    as state vs. federal responsibility, 212–215
Musk, Elon, 244

Native Alaskans, homeless, 3
Native Hawaiians, homeless, 3
Navigation Center, 268
New York City
    creation of shelter beds in, 255–256, 291–292
    failed approach of, 287–292
    lack of affordable housing in, 228, 256
NIMBY (not-in-my-backyard) phenomenon, 231–232, 241, 264, 278

Obama, Barack, 262
Obamacare (Affordable Care Act), 214
opportunity, unequal, 243
outpatient treatment, court-ordered, 282–286, 305

Pacific Islanders, homeless, 3
panhandling, 28
productivity, as American value, 241–243
public assistance, 24–26, 213–214

racism, 2–3, 240–241

"safety net," inadequacies of, 213–215, 250
San Francisco
    comparison of Trieste with, 292–301
    lack of affordable housing in, 225–226
    Proposition C ballot measure in, 258, 259
    shelter beds in, 232–233, 255, 257, 268
    vacancies in, 262
Section 8 vouchers, 231
segregation, 241
self-reliance, as American value, 241–243
shelters
    inadequacy of, 232–234, 251
    increasing number and quality of, 267–268, 302
    new form of, 268
    NIMBY resistance to, 231–232, 241
SRO (single-room occupancy) hotels, 216, 226, 228, 290
SSI (Supplemental Security Income), 24, 213, 223, 250
substance abuse treatment, 276, 303
success stories, 30, 255–260

Thorazine, 209
Trieste, Italy, comparison of San Francisco with, 292–301

ABOUT THE AUTHOR

Robert L. Okin, MD, was born in the Bronx, New York. He attended college and medical school at the University of Chicago, and after a psychiatric residency at the Albert Einstein College of Medicine in New York City, he spent two years at the National Institute of Mental Health, where he became interested in community psychiatry.

Early in his career, Dr. Okin was appointed commissioner of mental health for Vermont, and then for Massachusetts, where he led the development of community-based services for people who had previously spent years in public mental hospitals. He was one of the first commissioners to recognize the need for supportive housing for these people and to advocate for its creation.

A leading psychiatrist and internationally known expert on mental health service reform, Dr. Okin is a founding member of the board of advisors of Mental Disability Rights International (MDRI). He served as MDRI's lead psychiatric expert on technical assistance projects and investigative missions in Armenia, Azerbaijan, Hungary, Mexico, Paraguay, Peru, Romania, Turkey, and Ukraine.

Following the release of MDRI's report on Mexico in 2000, Dr. Okin served as an expert consultant to the Mexican government and helped close the abusive Ocaranza psychiatric facility in the state of Hidalgo, replacing it with more homelike settings and community-based services. In Paraguay, Dr. Okin helped MDRI negotiate a historic settlement agreement through the Inter-American Commission on Human Rights. As part of the settlement in 2005, Paraguay agreed to a number of improvements in its treatment of the mentally ill, including restructuring the national mental health service system, creating community services, and downsizing the country's main psychiatric facility.

Dr. Okin was chief of service of the San Francisco General Hospital Department of Psychiatry; professor of clinical psychiatry at the University of California, San Francisco; and vice chair of the University of California, San Francisco, School of Medicine's Department of Psychiatry, where he oversaw the development of crucial services for San Francisco's most acutely and chronically mentally ill patients, including the SFGH Department of Psychiatry's Emergency Department Case Management Program (which received the National Association of Public Hospitals and Health Systems' Safety Net Award in 1999).

As a world-recognized expert on human rights for the mentally disabled, Dr. Okin helped develop an international consensus statement condemning the use of electroconvulsive therapy without anesthesia. He has been quoted numerous times in the *New York Times*, was featured on ABC's *20/20* about his efforts to close down Ocaranza and help former residents live in the community, and has published numerous papers in psychiatric journals. In 2009, he received the American Psychiatric Association's prestigious Human Rights Award.

Dr. Okin lives in Northern California and has two grown children, Laura and Justin, and a young stepson, Oliver.